White Heat

White Heat

Edited with an introduction by

Patrick McGilligan

*Published for the Wisconsin Center for Film and Theater Research by
The University of Wisconsin Press*

Published 1984

The University of Wisconsin Press
114 North Murray Street
Madison, Wisconsin 53715

The University of Wisconsin Press, Ltd.
1 Gower Street
London WC1E 6HA England

Library of Congress Cataloging in Publication Data

Goff, Ivan.
White heat.

(Wisconsin/Warner Bros. screenplay series)
Screenplay prepared by Ivan Goff and Ben Roberts,
originally suggested by Virginia Kellogg.
Bibliography: p. 207.
I. Roberts, Ben. II. McGilligan, Patrick.
III. Kellogg, Virginia. IV. Title. V. Series.
PN1997.W5335 1984   791.43'72   83-40257
ISBN 0-299-09670-x cloth,
0-299-09674-2 paper

Contents

Foreword

In donating the Warner Film Library to the Wisconsin Center for Film and Theater Research in 1969, along with the RKO and Monogram film libraries and UA corporate records, United Artists created a truly great resource for the study of American film. Acquired by United Artists in 1957, during a period when the major studios sold off their films for use on television, the Warner library is by far the richest portion of the gift, containing eight hundred sound features, fifteen hundred short subjects, nineteen thousand still negatives, legal files, and press books, in addition to screenplays for the bulk of the Warner Brothers product from 1930 to 1950. For the purpose of this project, the company has granted the Center whatever publication rights it holds to the Warner films. In so doing, UA has provided the Center another opportunity to advance the cause of film scholarship.

Our goal in publishing these Warner Brothers screenplays is to explicate the art of screenwriting during the thirties and forties, the so-called Golden Age of Hollywood. In preparing a critical introduction and annotating the screenplay, the editor of each volume is asked to cover such topics as the development of the screenplay from its source to the final shooting script, differences between the final shooting script and the release print, production information, exploitation and critical reception of the film, its historical importance, its directorial style, and its position within the genre. He is also encouraged to go beyond these guidelines to incorporate supplemental information concerning the studio system of motion picture production.

We could set such an ambitious goal because of the richness of the script files in the Warner Film Library. For many film titles, the files might contain the property (novel, play, short story, or original story idea), research materials, variant drafts of scripts (from story outline to treatment to shooting script), post-production items such as press books and dialogue continuities, and legal records (details of the acquisition of the property, copyright registration, and contracts with actors and directors). Editors of the Wisconsin/Warner Bros. Screenplay Series receive copies of all the materials, along with prints of the films (the most authoritative ones available for reference purposes), to use in preparing the introductions and annotating the final shooting scripts.

In the process of preparing the screenplays for publication, typographical errors were corrected, punctuation and capitalization were modernized, and the format was redesigned to facilitate readability.

Unless otherwise specified, the photographs are frame enlargements taken from a 35-mm print of the film provided by United Artists.

In 1977 Warner Brothers donated the company's production records and distribution records to the University of Southern California and Princeton University, respectively. These materials are now available to researchers and complement the contents of the Warner Film Library donated to the Center by United Artists.

Tino Balio
General Editor

Introduction
"Made It, Ma! Top of the World!"

Patrick McGilligan

Among the countless gangster stories that have been cranked
out in Hollywood since the birth of cinema, few are as inge-
niously crafted or have such a chilling energy as *White Heat*. Its
star, James Cagney, was in the full vigor of his genius as an actor
and was making a comeback as a "tough guy" with the studio,
Warner Brothers, that had specialized in a tradition of gangster
pictures with an edge of social consciousness in the era of the
Great Depression. Its director, Raoul Walsh, was in top form
with an action assignment compatible with his strengths. And
White Heat had the advantage of a remarkable script that stands
today as a model of a certain type. It was written by two young
screenwriters, Ivan Goff and Ben Roberts, whose partnership
continues to prosper forty years after their initial collaboration.

Goff and Roberts, relative newcomers to the Warners stable in
1948, were aware of the studio's sympathetic gangster tradition,
but they were not bound by it. Indeed, they were of another
generation, more disillusioned and ambivalent (even about
something as sacrosanct as motherhood) in their social outlook.
They took Cagney—a leftist in his youth, a Republican for Dewey
by 1948—and deliberately created a part for him that would al-
ter and distort his early career image to symbolize everything
that had gone wrong with the world. True, the United States
had emerged a victor of World War II, but crippled veterans re-
turning home found a changed spirit in the land. FDR was dead

Introduction

and, with him, the "united front" atmosphere and visions of global democracy that so characterized the politics of the thirties; Stalin was no longer an ally and the hunt for Communists was under way in Hollywood as elsewhere throughout the nation.

Cynicism, despair, paranoia—these were postwar elements of the gangster genre popularized, if not wholly introduced, by *White Heat*. In the world of Goff and Roberts—as well as Cagney and Warners, now—there was less sanity, less compassion, less hope than in the thirties for a future in which technology and science were threatening additional Hiroshimas and Nagasakis (like the one symbolized by the incredible climax of their script).

The Story

Officially, the idea for the story of *White Heat* is credited to Virginia Kellogg, an ex-correspondent for the *Los Angeles Times* who turned to screenwriting in the 1930s. A stickler for journalistic authenticity, Kellogg wrote or originated the ideas for a number of grade-B movies, including *Mary Stevens, M.D.* (1933), *Stolen Holiday* (1936), *Meet the People* (1944), and *Screaming Eagles* (1956); she also worked on Ethyl Barrymore's anthology television series in the early fifties. *White Heat* was the most successful association of her career, apart from *Caged* (1950), a stark melodrama that Kellogg researched by incarcerating herself in women's prisons. For both *Caged* and its forerunner, *White Heat*, she received Academy Award nominations for Best Original Story, losing in both instances but benefiting from the prestige. Kellogg died in 1981.

A review of the material in the Warner library at the University of Wisconsin shows, however, that Kellogg's contribution was but the bare bones of an idea given its full dimension only after Warner Brothers purchased the story and yielded it to Goff and Roberts. According to her contract with the studio, Kellogg herself made use of research material by Fred C. Wasson when she initially marketed the story to an independent motion picture company associated with Warner Brothers, United States

10

Pictures, early in 1948.[1] When United States Pictures failed to launch the production, Kellogg renegotiated directly with Warners, which had a heritage of gangster pictures dating back to the silent era (and where her brother, Phil Kellogg, an agent, was a budding producer on the lot). Warners snapped up the idea in the spring of 1948 and signed Kellogg to a contract guaranteeing $2,000 for the story rights to *White Heat* plus five weeks of studio employment with an option for other ideas.

Kellogg wrote two thirty-page drafts that have survived in the Warners files—both quite different from the filmed *White Heat.* The earlier one, undated, sets the opening scene in a Washington, D.C., post office with the theft of new currency from the Bureau of Engraving and Printing. The focus of Kellogg's story, in this conception, is actually the Secret Service, "whose undercover activities are stranger than fiction" and to whom the prospective motion picture is dedicated. The first half of her story is devoted to a laborious field investigation by two federal officers—Hank Fallon, "a Walter Huston character, gnarled as the eagle he has served over forty years," and Vic Parker, a young "roper," or undercover ace—whose father-son relationship dominates the story line. Fallon's impending retirement provides the tension between these characters as they painstakingly dig for clues in St. Louis, Missouri, rumored to be the hideout city of the notorious Blackie Flynn gang.

It is not until Blackie Flynn surrenders—voluntarily, on a minor charge, as Cody Jarrett does in *White Heat*—that we even meet this Cody Jarrett prototype in Kellogg's original treatment. (Blackie, in fact, is somewhat overshadowed by the character of his wife, who is said to be "the brains of most capers.") Parker is assigned to ingratiate himself with Blackie and goes undercover, becoming Vic Pardo, a stickup specialist complete with false papers. Blackie and Parker are en route to prison when a

1. According to Ivan Goff, the head of United States Pictures was Milton Sperling, who was married to Harry Warner's daughter. Though its deal with Warner Brothers provided 100 percent financing, United States Pictures never produced anything of consequence, and, said Goff, "It was a big joke at the studio [Warner Brothers]." Sperling left the project when producer Lou Edelman came aboard.

two-car train, dubbed the Insane Express because its passengers are escaped lunatics being returned from California to Missouri, ominously crosses their path. Blackie's "orange eyes and cunning criminal features" narrow and he vows to Parker/Pardo, "They'd never get me on that one alive."

When Blackie's brother is killed during a caper, Blackie goes insane and manages to escape from prison with Parker, who is still undercover. His trail of murder and maniacal revenge leads Parker and the Secret Service to the elusive fence for the Blackie Flynn gang, an internationally renowned bridge expert who is in cahoots with a crooked insurance agent. At the moment of the climactic shoot-out with police, Blackie becomes mentally unhinged once and for all and pitches himself through an attic window onto a paved driveway below, crying, "They'll never get me on the Insane Express—alive!"

The plot line of the second Treatment, dated October 16, 1948, was not substantially altered. However, Kellogg moved the story to a western locale and gave it a more realistic, documentary flavor by patterning the opening-scene heist after the famous Denver Mint robbery of December 18, 1922, in which $200,000 in five-dollar Federal Reserve notes was stolen and one guard was killed. To this end, she appended factual notes and research on that robbery to her revised Treatment. Again, the emphasis in the story was on the two federal agents and their relationship. The St. Louis scenes were shifted to St. Paul, Minnesota, where, again, there is a dragnet for the gang on skid row, in fancy hotels, in sundry neighborhoods, and in the encircling wilderness.

This second Treatment ended Kellogg's involvement with the *White Heat* script. Elements of her original concept were, of course, retained for the film—particularly, the opening-scene heist, the "roper" character, the short-fused insanity of Blackie Flynn, and the shadowy fence who manipulates the Blackie Flynn gang. But these elements were so refashioned by Goff and Roberts as to become almost new—as in the case of the title, for example, which was inverted from its original meaning. Incredibly, Kellogg had called her story *White Heat* because, according to her Treatment, she felt the diligence of the Secret Service graphically illustrated the "white heat" of federal agents "driving themselves without rest or relays to track down the killers." This is hardly the implication of the title of the film, where "white heat," in the hands of Goff and Roberts, becomes a recurrent motif as represented by the scalding steam (of the opening-scene heist), the maddening headaches of Cody Jarrett, and the finale of the oil refinery explosion.

In interviews with this writer, Goff and Roberts said they scarcely remembered having seen the Kellogg Treatments. Although they later became quite friendly with Virginia Kellogg, they couldn't remember ever discussing her *White Heat* story with her. For the most part, they disregarded her Treatments in their script, retaining and layering upon her basic premise. If she was the architect of the house, they not only built it but interior-designed it and added a few wings and a porch. When she received story credit ("Suggested by a story by Virginia Kellogg") on the screen, they saw no reason to cavil. In those days, there was no clear financial edge to having the story credit, and no one was considering the eventuality of an Academy Award nomination, much less the recognitions of posterity. "But that credit was costly for us," admitted Goff in retrospect, ruefully.[2]

The Screenwriters

Ivan Goff is a transplanted Australian with experience as a reporter in Perth and, among other things, as a bookie in London. Ben Roberts is Bronx-born, a New York University graduate with a certificate in film and journalism. Their lives first crossed fleetingly at the old Republic Studios in Hollywood in the late thirties. Roberts had written Leon Errol and Edgar Kennedy two-reelers at RKO before teaming up at Republic with Sidney Sheldon (later the author of such best sellers as *The Other Side of Midnight, Bloodline,* and *Rage of Angels*). While they were marking time on a Mr. District Attorney picture, Goff was down the corridor working on a Three Mesquiters script for John Wayne.

2. I interviewed Ivan Goff and Ben Roberts in the summer and fall of 1981 in Los Angeles. All quotes attributed to them in this volume come from those sessions.

(Roberts said he and Sheldon used to wonder about this Goff fellow and whether, with his Aussie accent, he was writing such dialogue as "Head them off at the pass, chaps!")

With the onset of World War II, Roberts was drafted into the army, and he found himself stationed alongside Goff at the former Astoria Studios in Long Island churning out military propaganda short subjects. Sheldon followed Roberts to New York and they collaborated during off-time on the book for a Broadway revival of *The Merry Widow*. But soon, Sheldon returned to Hollywood and the partnership was dissolved, amicably. Still in the service, Roberts became well acquainted with Goff, and one day they sat down to have lunch together. Roberts had an idea for a short story that lacked an ending; Goff came up with the ending and suggested that they turn it into a play instead of a short story. That play, *Portrait in Black,* was their first joint effort, written at night over a period of thirteen months. It ran on Broadway, enjoyed some international vogue, and was twice sold to the movies (a version, starring Lana Turner, was made in 1960).

After their army hiatus and a seven-month attempt to write a

Ben Roberts (left) and Ivan Goff (right) in 1949, at work on White Heat.

comic play that failed to jell, the new team returned to Holly-wood and wrote their first motion picture, *The Shadow,* based on a Ben Hecht story. It took them fourteen days with the help of two secretaries. They still regard it as one of their finest collaborations, although, while optioned by many producers over the years, it has never been filmed. Warner Brothers hired them to rewrite a script that wasn't working, *Backfire,* a missing-persons mystery directed by Vincent Sherman and populated by the then–stock company of Virginia Mayo, Edmond O'Brien, Viveca Lindfors, and Gordon MacRae. It turned out better than anyone had expected, and Goff and Roberts were signed to a five-year studio contract. They regarded themselves as writers of high comedy; on the evidence of their work on the *Backfire* screenplay (the film was ultimately released in 1950), the studio considered them to be pretty fair action writers, and Steve Trilling, then head of production, assigned them to *White Heat.* Roberts recalled the initial sessions:

> They [Warners executives] wanted to do a gangster story, and they gave us some material written by Virginia Kellogg about the Denver Mint robbery. We said, "We don't want to do this. It's simply a bank robbery. It's ordinary, conventional, banal." They said, "What would you like to do?" We said, "We don't know. Give us some time to think about it." So we thought about it and we synthesized Ma Barker down to having the one son instead of four, and we put the evil of all four into one man. Then we went back and said, "We'd like to do Ma Barker and have the gangster with a mother complex and play it against Freudian implications that she's driving him to do these things, and he's driving himself to self-destruction. Play it like a Greek tragedy." They said, "Fellas . . . ?" We said, "Believe us, it will work. And there's only one man who can play this and make the rafters rock. That is Jimmy Cagney."

From Trilling came the response: Jack Warner would not agree to have Cagney back on the payroll. "They fight like pit bulls," explained Trilling. (According to Goff, Warner is said to have exclaimed at one point, "I wouldn't have that little bastard back on the lot!") Cagney and Warner were age-old adversaries, dating back to the studio's feudal treatment of Cagney in the early thirties. According to Goff, "Jimmy, who was raised in a part of New York, one of the Irish blocks that was cheek-by-jowl with

15

the Jewish blocks, knew some Yiddish, and if J.L. would come down on a set and bitch about something, Jimmy would abuse him in Yiddish." When Cagney left Warner Brothers after the triumph of *Yankee Doodle Dandy* (1942), he had vowed never to return; Jack Warner had vowed, likewise, never to take him back. But the screenwriters persisted in their argument. "*White Heat* cried for Warners and it cried for Cagney," explained Goff. And the commercial prospects of a "tough guy" comeback were finally too great for both Cagney and Jack Warner to ignore. Cagney signed.

With Cagney set for the leading role, work on the script progressed in earnest. A producer was assigned to the project: Lou Edelman, a Warners contract producer who had supervised *Backfire* and whose subsequent career was to include involvement in television with "Wyatt Earp," "Make Room for Daddy," and "The Big Valley." The first draft was six months in gestation. Goff and Roberts regard themselves as slow, methodical craftsmen. They plot in complete detail before even beginning to write. Then they write their dialogue together, line by line. Roberts seems to be the better constructionist; an omnivorous reader, he probably introduced the classical underpinnings of the *White Heat* plot. Goff gets the nod for detail and dialogue. Yet they work together so closely that it is difficult to separate their individual contributions, and what usually emerges is a blending of both their selves. "Our contention, and I think it's borne out by the scripts we've done," said Roberts, "is that the style of the script is neither my style nor Ivan's, but a third person's."

The Script

In addition to the Kellogg Treatments, five drafts of the Goff and Roberts version of *White Heat* survive in the Warners archives: Treatment (dated November 9, 1948); Temporary (March 10, 1949); Revised Temporary (April 8, 1949); Final (April 20, 1949); and Revised Final (May 4–June 18, 1949). Aside from some departures from the Revised Final—especially in Cagney's dialogue—the film is strikingly faithful to the script. In part, this is because the story was so intelligently honed over the course of the various drafts—but many of the essential and now familiar aspects of the movie were in place, recognizably, from the first Goff-Roberts treatment.

Initially, Goff and Roberts clung somewhat to the manhunt drama that was so key to Kellogg's version and to the precarious relationship between the characters Hank Fallon and Philip Evans (who are vaguely identified at this point in the writing as being either FBI, Secret Service, or Treasury agents). Evans's marriage—and his wife—is given scrutiny, as is the trauma of his impending retirement. Emphasis is on "the thoroughness, the modernity" of law-enforcement agencies by spotlighting "the newest technical and mechanical devices for the apprehension of criminals," notably, spectroscopic analysis (whereby a man's clothing can be analyzed for dust); the "snooperscope," which utilizes infrared ray technique for seeing in darkness; and signal devices clamped beneath a car that send out electrical impulses to FBI receiving machines.

"But more than this [the angle of the manhunt] even," the screenwriters noted in the Treatment, "it is a story of personalities, of people, of human courage and human frailty, of ruthless depradation and murder, and of love and kindness. To illustrate, there is the relationship between a young nerveless G-man (Hank Fallon) and his superior (Philip Evans), divisional field chief, in our area of operations. Once Evans was as nerveless as Fallon, but 15 years of tracking down criminals has left dents in the steel shell of his composure. The Evans-Fallon relationship forms the basis for the foreground story, told on the top level, during the relentless search for the men who robbed the armored car of a train grinding across the Rockies toward San Francisco."

Thus, the Cody Jarrett (neé Blackie Flynn) current of the story was relegated to the background. Yet the main dramatic ingredients of the film were already conspicuous in Goff and Roberts's first version, which unfolded in three distinct acts like a well-made stage play. The first act encompassed the bloody heist now set outside a railroad tunnel in the Rockies (based on the actual holdup of a mail train in the low Sierras); as well as the depiction of Cody's sympathy-inducing headaches, his "mother complex," and the "incipient paranoia and fear of his rapacious and stone-hearted mother, Ma Jarrett, that one day her son's mind will snap, as his father's did." The second act centered on Cody's stretch in prison, covering the relationship between Fallon and Cody; the conspiracy between "Big Ed" Somers and Jarrett's wife, Verna; and the killing of Ma that triggers Cody's vengeful escape. The screenwriters needed a "topper," or climactic sequence, for *White Heat* and they hit upon the solution while scouting locations around Los Angeles. The swirling pipes, retorts, Hortonspheres, coils, and tubes of a sprawling oil refinery suggested "mother earth in metal" (in Goff's words) and inspired the third act, which included the ABC technology of police surveillance (a tailing method not yet in wide use), the abortive "Trojan horse" payroll robbery at a southern California oil-cracking plant, and Cody's spectacular demise.

Gone, in this Treatment, were Kellogg's scenes in either St. Louis or St. Paul. Goff and Roberts switched the locales to California (for the opening-scene heist) and Tulsa, Oklahoma (for the prison scenes). Among the curious details that the writers toyed with and then abandoned in subsequent drafts: Fallon's skin is "pigment-bleached to the shade befitting a man who has been incarcerated from arrest through conviction"; Verna divorces Cody while he is in prison and marries Big Ed; Cody is almost knifed to death in prison (not crushed by heavy-duty machinery, as in the film); an actress named Margaret Baxter is employed by Evans to impersonate Fallon/Pardo's wife and to carry messages to him in prison; after the prison breakout, Cody kills Big Ed in a "taut gun duel" in Riverside, Calif.; Bo Creel is a full-fledged member of the Jarrett gang who is always staring searchingly at Fallon/Pardo ("Hasn't he seen Pardo somewhere before?"); when Fallon/Pardo asks Cody if he can see his "wife," it is Bo Creel who flies to Denver and brings the undercover actress to the Jarrett gang hideout; not Cody's death but a romantic fade-out between Fallon and Margaret Baxter concludes the story.

By the time the Temporary script was finished four months later, the focus had definitely shifted to the Jarretts—Cody, Ma, and Verna. The scenes between Evans and Fallon, and between

Fallon and a superior of Evans's named Penneman (scenes which take place in Washington, D.C.), are still in the story, as are the scenes between Evans and Mary (Evans's wife), and between Evans and the undercover actress. But the recharged emphasis is on the personality and behavior of Cody ("Leader of the Jarrett mob, arrogant, devoid of fear or conscience, yet with a neurotic dependence on his mother"), Ma Jarrett ("The founders of Mother's Day would have reconsidered it quickly if they had ever met Ma Jarrett"), and Verna ("Her face is beautiful but about as warm as the snow that edges the windows—and about as permanent. Verna's philosophy is simple: What's in it for Verna?"). The bond between Cody and Ma is too sentimental, too obviously neurotic at this stage of the writing, but Cody's ruthlessness begins to emerge as the compelling factor of the plot's momentum. And much of the unforgettable character incident of the movie is already in the script (for example, the vignette of Cody matter-of-factly shooting a stooge through the trunk of a car makes its appearance in the Temporary script).

The Revised Temporary, completed within a month, moved still further in the direction of the film's final form. Still, there were complications: Cody's surrender to local arrest is preceded by a teary farewell scene with Ma and Verna at a night-cloaked airplane hangar, a lapse into maudlinity that was eventually dropped. The Evans-Fallon-Penneman subplot is still very much in evidence, though Evans's wife has vanished. The Trader, an international fence who is the purported mastermind of the Jarrett gang, is introduced midway in the story and is blithely informed by Big Ed that Cody will soon be killed off in prison. The Margaret Baxter subplot is still in favor, and her conversations with Fallon ring with sexual double entendre.

The Final script (Part II of which was never completed) and the Revised Final resolved the plotting. The subplot of Evans's impending retirement is finally abandoned. Fallon doesn't enter the storyline until after Cody Jarrett's confession to a crime he did not commit. The prison scenes are set in Illinois. The character of Bo Creel is used sparingly and more strategically. The Trader is deprived of his early appearance in the story and doesn't crop up until the "third act." Ma Jarrett reigns over the Jarrett

gang in Cody's absence—an important, motivating plot element. The shiv attack on Cody becomes a near-fatal "accident"
involving a metal transformer—a good change of detail and one
that proved to be more cinematic. Verna is integrated into the
scenes leading up to the oil refinery climax. The romance-tinged
subplot involving "actress" Margaret Baxter is virtually eliminated. (Calendar dates on some of the pages of the Revised Final indicate that the screenwriters, working against the clock,
made some of these final modifications as filming progressed
during May and June 1949.)

James Cagney

Who would disagree that *White Heat* boasts one of Cagney's most
eccentric and brilliant performances? No one, except perhaps
Cagney himself. It is not a movie by which he has ever cared to
be remembered. In his autobiography, he describes the picture
as a "cheapjack job" and complains that the powers-that-be ig-
nored his recommendation for casting old pal Frank McHugh as
Jarrett gang member Tommy Ryley. "The original script of *White
Heat* was very formula," he adds. "The old knock-down-drag-
'em-out again, without a touch of imagination or originality."[3]
This is all the more ironic considering that Goff and Roberts were
practically the only screenwriters over whom Cagney ever waxed
enthusiastic (apart from John Bright and Kubec Glasmon, who
wrote *Public Enemy* and other Cagney vehicles in the early thirties, and twin brothers Philip G. and Julius J. Epstein, who
"doctored" *Yankee Doodle Dandy*). He employed Goff and Roberts for three other pictures in the twilight of his career: *Come,
Fill the Cup* (1951), *Man of a Thousand Faces* (1957) (for which they

3. James Cagney, *Cagney by Cagney* (Garden City, N.Y.: Doubleday, 1976), p.
125. Also in his autobiography, Cagney claims credit for turning Cody Jarrett
into "a psychotic to account for his actions" and for fashioning Ma Jarrett after
Ma Barker "for some kind of variant." Nowhere does he mention the contributions of Goff and Roberts. Though it is unusual for Cagney to be so self-
congratulatory about a script, his memory does not stand up against the evidence of the various script drafts, and in all probability he was exaggerating his
own input to emphasize—belatedly—his dislike for the gangster story *White
Heat*.

received an Oscar nomination for Best Story and Screenplay), and *Shake Hands with the Devil* (1959), among Cagney's finest films of the fifties.

His attitude toward *White Heat* can best be appreciated in context. Cagney spent a lifetime resisting his "tough guy" image by rising above the "hell's kitchen" of his childhood and later by fighting the gangster typecasting that dogged him after he smashed a grapefruit into the face of Mae Clarke in *Public Enemy* (1931). A sensitive artist and a reclusive celebrity, he preferred to think of himself as a song-and-dance man, for indeed that is how, in vaudeville, he entered show business and the acting profession. Time and again over the span of his career he was saddled with the roles of young punks and aging hoodlums. Some of these movies were personally objectionable to him, and many of them he never cared to watch, even once. Later, in retirement, he said that he never watched his old movies when they turned up on television, except for the handful of musicals whose memory he relished. He would rather have been playing a Hamlet or a Eugene O'Neill character than a Cody Jarrett.

Though *White Heat* signaled a triumphant comeback for him in the minds of some critics and audiences, it could not help but seem a concession to him at the time. After winning the Oscar for Best Actor for his performance in *Yankee Doodle Dandy* (1942), Cagney and his brother William (his closest adviser and frequent producer) broke away from Warner Brothers and set up a family company, Cagney Productions, with the announced ambition of counteracting Cagney's gangster image. Freed of Jack Warner, the Cagneys mounted three films in the next six years, among them Cagney's most personal and evocative works: a whimsical adaptation of Louis Bromfield's *Johnny Come Lately* (1943) and a version of William Saroyan's *The Time of Your Life* (1948). (The third picture, *Blood on the Sun*, in 1945, was a more formulaic melodrama, pitched to World War II patriotism.) But the independent Cagney Productions proved a failure economically. The struggling outfit had to deal with Hollywood disapproval, poor distribution, legal entanglements, and persistent financial difficulty. In 1948, Cagney had to accept a free-lance assignment in Henry Hathaway's *13 Rue Madeleine*. By 1949, after production costs had soared on *The Time of Your Life,* Cagney's career needed a boost and Cagney Productions needed operating income. Hence, *White Heat* beckoned. Significantly, provisions were made in Cagney's fifty-seven-page contract (which guaranteed him $250,000 per picture for three pictures over the next three years) for the production and distribution through Warners of one independent Cagney Productions feature for every Warners release.[4]

Yet Cagney's hindsight observations do not reflect the fact that the *White Heat* script generated much excitement at the Warner Brothers studio in 1949 and that Cagney approached it at the time with appreciation and enthusiasm. He knew it would revitalize his career. Roberts recalled:

> When he came into the project, he just came to our office once. He lay down on the couch, like he always did, and he said, "What are you going to do, fellas?" We said, "Jimmy, we're going to keep it moving, and we're going to make him [Cody Jarrett] a really interesting character—the study of an evil man—but we want the audience to understand *why* he is evil. We see that behind his state of cruelty is a man who is driven, who is really sick, who is driving himself toward destruction. We don't want to compare ourselves with Greek tragedians but it is, in a sense, about a man who is destined to die, who knows it, and who wants to get where he wants to go before it happens. Everyone that is in his way is thrust aside, and ruthlessly." Cagney said, "Well, it sounds interesting. Sounds like it will be fun to play." We said, "We'll give you some scenes to play that we think will be pretty hairy." He said, "Whatever you say, fellas!" Jimmy was marvelous that way. It was always like that with him on the pictures we did with him. He would say, "What are you going to do, fellas?" Then, "Whatever you say, fellas!"

Cast and Crew

The remaining roles in *White Heat* were filled by Warner Brothers contract players, with one exception: Ma Jarrett was played by Margaret Wycherly, widow of playwright Bayard Veiller and

4. See Patrick McGilligan, *Cagney: The Actor as Auteur* (A. S. Barnes/Tantivy Press, 1975; Da Capo, 1980), for additional background on Cagney Productions and the themes of Cagney's career. See also Patrick McGilligan, *Cagney,* revised

mother of Warners producer Anthony Veiller. The London-born
Wycherly was, in her day, one of the great stars of the legitimate
theater, with extensive Shakespearean and Shavian credits as
well as a considerable career in later years as a character actress
in film and on television. (When she died in 1956 at the age of
74, her *Variety* obituary did not even mention *White Heat*.) Ex–
Goldwyn Girl Virginia Mayo, who had come to fame as an in-
genue in the years immediately following World War II, was cast
as Verna. Edmond O'Brien, whose Shakespearean roles on
Broadway had led to a Hollywood contract, was picked as Hank
Fallon. Ex-cowpuncher, ex-railroad hand, ex-fireman, ex-shipyard
worker, and ex-hobo Steve Cochran played Big Ed Somers, a
"tough guy" characterization in which he specialized, off-screen
as well as on, during a career that ended with his mysterious
death at sea off the coast of Guatemala in 1965. Veteran actor
Fred Clark played the Trader.

The director was to be Raoul Walsh, a logical choice among
the contract directors and, as it turned out, an inspired one. A
"rough diamond," in the words of screenwriter Goff, Walsh was
a colorful figure who had roamed the West and ridden with Pan-
cho Villa before launching his career in movies with D. W. Grif-
fith, first as an actor impersonating John Wilkes Booth in *Birth
of a Nation* (1917), then as a prolific director.[5] One of his eyes was
patched in black as the result of a freak accident during the
shooting of *The Big Trail* (1930), the first "talkie" western. Though
he rarely looked through the camera, he had an instinctive visual flair and was an unpretentious, compelling storyteller. At
Warners intermittently in the thirties and steadily throughout
the forties, Walsh had directed Cagney before, notably in *The
Roaring Twenties* (1939) opposite Humphrey Bogart and in the
turn-of-the-century comedy-drama *The Strawberry Blonde* (1941),
proving to be one of Cagney's most vital and understanding di-

and updated edition (A. S. Barnes, 1982). See also Patrick McGilligan, ed., *Yankee Doodle Dandy,* Wisconsin/Warner Bros. Screenplay Series (Madison: University of Wisconsin Press, 1981).

5. See Raoul Walsh's autobiography, *Each Man in His Time* (New York: Farrar,
Straus & Giroux, 1974), for a rambling, first-hand account of this moviemaker's
full and exciting life.

rectors. Walsh excelled at themes of romantic history and manly adventure, and his strongest period of work during the sound era occurred at Warners in the forties, where he directed the male heroes of the lot—Bogart, Cagney, and Errol Flynn—in pictures like *The Roaring Twenties, They Drive by Night* (1940), *The Strawberry Blonde, High Sierra* (1941), *They Died with Their Boots On* (1941), *Gentleman Jim* (1942), and *White Heat.* Conversely, his movies suffered if the heroines were a bit too vapid and Walsh grew disinterested in them. "You see," he once explained, "I was brought up with a rough crowd in Texas and Montana when I was young, and I guess it kind of stuck with me to like strong women."[6] Ma Jarrett and Verna, two of the more peculiar heroines in movie annals, appealed to his interest. "Men were his strength," remembered Goff, "and it was possibly better for him that the girl in *White Heat* was a bad girl and the mother was the mother of a bad guy."

Walsh's cameraman for *White Heat* was Sidney Hickox, who entered the industry in 1915 as an assistant cameraman with American Biograph and spent most of his career at Warner Brothers perfecting the graphic, newsreel-like "studio look." Hickox had shot other Cagney films in the thirties; he had worked with directors George Cukor and Frank Borzage and with Walsh on *Gentleman Jim;* but the cinematography of *White Heat,* "which looks as though he deliberately stained the camera with sand pebbles," in the words of screenwriter Roberts, is one of the high points of his list of titles, a superbly realized expression of darkness and criminality. Warners craftsmen Owen Marks and Edward Carrere served as editor and art director, respectively. The agitato musical score was by the ever-reliable Max Steiner.

The Filming

According to Warner Brothers publicity, there are 260 separate scenes in *White Heat* (and, for trivia buffs, thirteen violent deaths).

6. Patrick McGilligan, Debra Weiner, and Dix Bruce, "Raoul Walsh Remembers Warners," *The Velvet Light Trap,* No. 15 (Fall 1975), p. 42.

Mayo and director Walsh during a break in filming.

The opening scenes were filmed in the rugged Santa Susana Mountains near Chatsworth, California, using a Southern Pacific railroad tunnel and train for three days. The mountain hideaway scenes and the lodge setting of the "third act" were shot in the "back vastness" of the Warner Brothers ranch, near Calabasas, California. The prison scenes were shot in Warners' own authentically styled steel cellblock, patterned after San Quentin, Folsom, and other California prisons and recognizable in many other Warners features. The studio machine shop was used for the filming of the mess hall scene. The climax was filmed in the industrial district south of Los Angeles, near Torrance and the Signal Hill oil wells, on the grounds of one of southern California's largest chemical and oil refinery plants.

The Revised Final was followed closely not only in its dialogue content but also in its visual scheme. The most indelible moments of *White Heat*—Cody being comforted by Ma, Cody's prison freak-out, the fiery climax—are all taken practically shot-for-shot from the Goff-Roberts screenplay. To Walsh's credit, he valued the script and embraced it wholeheartedly and—with the exception of one minor scene—filmed it as it was devised.

At the same time, Cagney's interpolations, or "touches," as he was so fond of calling his contributions to a script or characterization, were evident throughout the film. These touches were subtle but precise. Indeed they confirm how instinctively he inhabited the role of Cody Jarrett and, whatever later protestations to the contrary, how deeply involved he was in the story.

The moment in which Cody Jarrett sits on Ma Jarrett's lap, which is not in the screenplay, is a case in point. It may be that Raoul Walsh suggested this perfect bit of business, as Walsh sometimes claimed in later interviews, although Walsh was scarcely renowned for such nuances. It is more likely that Cagney, as was his wont, improvised the gesture on the set, thereby beautifully underscoring the Oedipus complex of Cody Jarrett. Cagney explains, "To get in the Ma Barker flavor with some pungency, I thought we would try something, take a little gamble. Cody Jarrett is psychotically tied to his mother's apron strings. I wondered if we dare have him sit in her lap once for comfort. I said to the director, Raoul Walsh, 'Let's see if we can get away with this.' He said, 'Let's try it.' We did, and it worked."[7]

However the scene evolved, it did work, and Cagney is one of the very few male stars who would have attempted it or could have carried it off. For one thing, dating back to his debut film, *Sinner's Holiday* in 1930, having a "mother" who roots for him was an essential part of Cagney's screen persona and the actor understood why as well as his screenwriters: for audience sympathy. As Roberts recalled, "Jimmy stopped by the office one day [after filming] and said, "I just did something startling. I don't know if it will work. Raoul thinks it will." We said, 'What did you do?' He said, 'I sat on Mama's lap.' We just looked at each other and thought it'll be sensational if it works. Without saying anything, it's what the picture is about—the Oedipal thing. He reverts to the child who needs his mother. Then when we saw it on film, it was marvelous, because it was so simply done."

7. Cagney, *Cagney by Cagney*, p. 126.

Added Goff, "The audiences [of the time] were startled but they knew they were looking at something awfully personal. And it was a great moment because of that."

At various key junctures of the narrative, other Cagney touches accented Cody Jarrett's cruelty and perverse vulnerability on the subject of Ma. When it was suitable, he played a scene one notch higher (or more *in extremis*) than it was written, adding just a simple twist that triggered another shade of meaning or reaction. The brief scene, for example, in which Verna tells Cody that Ma has gone off in search of strawberries for her gangster son ends unsatisfactorily in the Revised Final with Cody giving Verna a withering look. On the set it just wasn't enough. Walsh stopped the cameras and asked Cagney for a "topper." Cagney suggested knocking Verna down, but Walsh thought better of it—too cliche. Then Cagney suggested that Verna be standing on a chair, which Cody kicks out from under her after her sarcastic remark. And that is the way the scene unravels in *White Heat*—a small detail that helps make an otherwise unimportant scene click.

How to convey the mental deterioration of Cody Jarrett was a problem that Cagney, carrying through the intentions of the script, resolved with sensitivity and daring. The "third act" nighttime interlude on the edge of the forest near the Jarrett gang hideout, with Cody's feeling soliloquy about the ghost of Ma, was played with haunting intimacy. Again, audiences were caught off-guard by the emotion and seduced even as they were, perhaps, horrified. As in his earlier scenes with Margaret Wycherly, Cagney veered away from the literal screenplay a bit, flavoring the dialogue with his own phraseology, going with the flow of his inspiration. "That he'll do all the time," acknowledged screenwriter Roberts. "When he feels something he just keeps going, and it's usually very good."

Cagney's feeling for the material was likewise "very good" during the scene in which Cody, surrounded by legions of armed police, suffers his final burst of insanity atop the Hortonsphere at the refinery. In the film, Cody is giggling and shrieking with mad laughter as he is brought down by a hail of bullets and an explosion of fire. That bizarre element—the mirth of Cody Jarrett as he self-destructs—is not in the script. The giggling and the laughter were among Cagney's touches on the set—yet another detail that somehow magnificently caps the movie.

Probably the most unforgettable scene in *White Heat* takes place in the prison mess hall when Cody Jarrett, learning of Ma's betrayal and death, goes uncontrollably berserk. Ironically, that scene was almost taken out of the script, for it was one of two scenes that Jack Warner found fault with, for budgetary reasons.[8] (The other, a wintry scene in the "first act" at the Jarrett gang hideaway, was supposedly too costly because of the scripted snow, so the snow was cut.) Warner summoned the screenwriters, producer Edelman, and director Walsh to his office and complained about the exorbitant costs of a single scene with six hundred extras and only one line of dialogue. According to Roberts,

Jack called us in and he said, "The script's pretty good but it's expensive. That scene in the mess hall—can you play it in the chapel?" We said, "Jack, what's Cody Jarrett doing in the chapel? Praying? And secondly, the whole point of the scene is to have a lot of noise that goes absolutely dead silent when he makes his first animal-like scream. All the rattling knives and forks suddenly go dead silent—that's the terror of the scene. It'll make the hair on your scalp prickle. But if you put it in the chapel, it'll already be quiet because nobody will be saying anything." As I recall, Raoul Walsh finally said, "Give me three hundred extras and the machine shop, which we'll convert into a mess hall, and we'll be out by noon so the men can go back to work." Warner said, "You've got it." So Walsh did it in three hours and was out for lunch. One take.

Before shooting the mess hall scene, Cagney consulted with the screenwriters, asking, "How crazy do you want that?" According to Roberts, "We said, 'You're the actor, Jimmy, we just put it down on paper. If you make people's spines tingle, so much the better.'" Still, no one was quite sure of the level at which he was going to play the scene, since Cagney was not known for being voluble about his "method." The writers, Wil-

8. Said Goff, "J.L. seldom came up with a story idea except perhaps to save a buck or two."

liam Cagney, and others were on the set for a day that everyone suspected would be worth remembering. Cagney walked through his planned paces for Walsh, who covered him with several cameras. Then, on cue, he transformed himself, becoming as crazed as a beast. It was—and is, on film—terrifying and credible. It is said that the extras, not prepared for what was about to happen, were stunned and for an instant truly believed they had just seen a famous actor go insane. Within minutes, Cagney was off-camera, relaxed and joking, and wearing taps on his shoes for the buck-and-wings he practiced during breaks.[9]

Though it may be rare for screenwriters to be so satisfied with the rendering of their script, Goff and Roberts are fond of the memory of the filming of *White Heat* and are proud of the finished work, which is as true as possible to the authors' design. They have only one quibble about Raoul Walsh's direction, and about that minor scene—the whispering scene between Cody and Fallon in their prison cell in which Cody reveals his intentions to escape—the two screenwriters, in fact, disagree. In the script the scene is intercut between the two characters. On the set Walsh had it set up with a master and several other accompanying shots. Cagney suggested playing it in one "take" without any camera movement, saying, according to Roberts, "What are you doing that for, Raoul? That's a lot of movement. The camera's going to jerk around. This is supposed to be a confidential scene. Why don't you just start back and move in and we'll just play the whole scene?" Walsh deferred to Cagney and

9. In his autobiography Cagney writes, "Not long ago a reporter asked me if I didn't have to 'psych' myself up for the scene in *White Heat* where I go berserk on learning of my mother's death. My answer to the question is that you don't psych yourself up for these things, you do them. I can imagine what some of the old-timers would have said in answer to that question. They would have laughed aloud at the idea of an actor pumping himself up with emotional motivations to do a scene. The pro is supposed to know what to do, then go ahead and do it. In this particular scene, I knew what deranged people sounded like because once as a youngster I had visited Ward's Island where a pal's uncle was in the hospital for the insane. My God, what an education that was! The shrieks, the screams of those people under restraint! I remembered those cries, saw that they fitted, and I called on my memory to do as required. No need to psych up" (p. 126).

played the scene, intimately, with one close-in camera. "It worked," said Goff, "but it would have been better if it was done with more conventional cutting. Elements of the drama were not punctuated properly because of that." Roberts disagreed, saying, "It was much better [as filmed], because it kept us riveted to those two guys."

The Film

Even after so many years have passed and after a revolution in filmmaking values has taken place, one must admire the screenplay, as filmed, of *White Heat*. The relationships are captured in a line or gesture; the outlaw subculture is wholly believable; seeds planted in one "act" pay off in another; there is symmetry (Ma Jarrett and surrogate Ma Hank Fallon, fisherman manque Fallon and fisherman poseur The Trader); there is the recurrent "white heat" motif; and there are the classical rumblings—the Achilles' heel of Cody Jarrett's headaches, his Oedipus complex, the Trojan horse robbery (with its double-edged theme of Fallon as an impostor in the belly of the Jarrett gang).[10] As written and as filmed, this richly nuanced story is a paragon of screenwriting craftsmanship.

Apart from its construction, *White Heat* is also a story that made dramaturgical inroads for the gangster genre. For one thing, it was one of a series of movies, beginning perhaps with John Huston's film of W. R. Burnett's *High Sierra* in 1941, that shifted the locale of the gangster jungle from the urban East to the snow-capped mountains and arid desert terrain of the West—with the dying frontier becoming another variation on the "dead end." As such, it influenced movies and literature for years to come.[11]

10. Were the classical nuances deliberate or, as the screenwriters insist, partly subconscious? According to Goff, "That [the several elements of Greek tragedy] was just a couple of screenwriters working hard to make things look different, that's all." Said Roberts, who was schooled in the classics and whose personal library is stocked with classical literature: "I'm not even sure it was intentional, although what you are as a human being comes out in your writing subconsciously, regardless."

11. Commenting on the shift of the gangster environ to the West in *White Heat*, Goff added this interesting observation: "We never thought of it as a gang-

Introduction

The degree of violence was unusual, as was a gangster whose insanity or criminality was psychologically oriented. Warner Brothers had always stressed the street-corner, sociological roots of its gangster archetypes. Other films of the era, notably *Kiss of Death* in 1947, promoted gangster heroes who were equally deranged, reflecting the general postwar letdown in America; but *White Heat*, especially because of Cagney's previous status as an "everyman" in movies like *The Public Enemy*, had a more significant impact.[12]

Of course, there *are* gaps in the script and in the film. Some of the early wrinkles in the script's development plagued the finished picture: the Treasury agents, for example, come across as mechanical, dull, and a trifle unsympathetic, too much of the life having been drained out of them in the various rewrites. The Hank Fallon character, while convincingly enacted by Edmond O'Brien, suffers in this vein; he could have been written (or directed) with a little more coloration. For example, his stubborn lack of empathy toward Cody, who befriends him, removes from the story what might have been another level of conflict and emotion. Cody Jarrett's graceful leap from the top of a tunnel onto a speeding train is improbable. The ABC tracking and surveillance technology of the police may have been exciting at the time, but nowadays it is the most dated aspect of the film.

Yet these are minor fault-findings that do not weigh heavily on the reputation or merit of a widely acknowledged "classic." *White Heat* is one of those rare Hollywood instances in which everything coalesced: studio, script, cast, crew, director. Margaret Wycherly's portrayal is weird and driven, oddly affecting; Virginia Mayo has never been as icy or as transparent. O'Brien, Cochran, and Clark deliver solid performances. Cagney, of course, played it to the hilt. The vulnerability as well as the ruthlessness

---

ster film, or of Cody as a gangster. It had, in fact, much more of an *outlaw* feeling for us. Gangsters are mobsters, have mob muscle and back-up and 'connections.' Bandits, in our book, had to do it all on their own, as they had from Wild West days." At one point in a script draft, the screenwriters actually described Cody Jarrett as "the last outlaw."

12. See Andrew Bergman's sociological film survey, *We're in the Money: Depression America and Its Films* (New York: Harper and Colophon, 1972).

of Cody Jarrett he understood, and both were given unbridled intensity and conviction. Whether Cagney himself liked it or not, it remains one of his hallmark performances—just as it remains one of director Walsh's most exceptional efforts. "*White Heat* was his [Walsh's] kind of film," noted screenwriter Roberts. "It was all visceral, driven, and all the subtle character points didn't have to be examined, because Jimmy wasn't examining them. Jimmy was acting as if they were on the surface, but we hoped when you saw the film you would see the whole history of the man. Walsh just wanted to drive it home and make it look real and that he did."

When the picture opened in movie theaters in August and September of 1949, the initial reviews were cautious: praise for the production values of the movie, certainly, and for Cagney's blistering performance, but tempered by complaints that the movie was insidiously or unnecessarily violent. "For two hours in *White Heat* you are subjected to an unending procession of what is probably the most gruesome aggregation of brutalities ever presented upon the motion picture screen under the guise of entertainment," wrote the reviewer for *Cue*. "Brilliantly directed," wrote James Agee in *Time*. "A wild and exciting mixture of mayhem and madness," said *Life*. "The old Jimmy is back again."

Typical of the soul-searching among critics was the response of Bosley Crowther of the *New York Times*, whose initial review on September 3, 1949, called *White Heat* "the acme of the gangster-prison film" with a "brilliantly graphic" portrayal by Cagney. One week later, Crowther took the unusual step of writing a second, revised opinion, this time calling Cagney's comeback role

ironic and just a little sad. It isn't sad, mind you, from the viewpoint of the avid thriller fans—nor from the point of view of the Warners, who will reap a vast harvest with this film. . . . For the innocent thrills and amusement—yes, amusement—which a well-designed *White Heat* can give to large segments of the public are balanced, we feel sure, by the unhealthy stimulation which such a film affords the weak and young. And the notions it spreads of moral values are dangerously volatile. For inevitably Mr. Cagney, bold and indomitable, appears a remarkable hero in this modern-jungle film. He loves his mother, he is scrupulously loyal to the best interest of his gang, he is brave, he detests a two-timer and he won't compromise with the law. The irony of his brief existence, as it seems at the last to be revealed, is not that he took to killing because of misguided youth but that, in his grief and desolation, he was outsmarted by a clever cop. We heard a kid in the audience at the Strand the other day greet one of his vicious capers with a rhapsodic "Bee-you-tee-ful!" The echo rang grim and horrendous in that youngster-packed theatre.

An interesting dissent of a different sort was filed by John Howard Lawson, one of the Hollywood Ten. Lawson saw *White Heat* while he was incarcerated in a federal prison for his refusal to testify before the House Un-American Activities Committee about the role of the Communist Party in Hollywood. Later, Lawson wrote intriguingly about the social message of the gangster figure:

Hollywood produces films which cover a wide variety of subject-matter and setting. But a major trend in the past five years has been the growing emphasis on sex and murder (or attempted murder and attempted sex) as thematic material.

There is a similar trend in radio and television, in books, magazines, and in the comic strips. The cycle of pornography and gangsterism gives a false picture of American life, and tends to blunt the moral sense of the audience. The portrayal of brutes and sadists as "attractive" figures, and even as "heroes," is connected with the war drive. The connection becomes clear as the earlier pattern of sex and violence evolves toward direct propaganda for war and fascist regimentation.

The "simple" theme of murder presented as entertainment is exemplified in *White Heat*, in which James Cagney starred in 1949. Cagney plays the part of a psychopathic killer who commits six or eight murders—some of them bloody acts of unmotivated fury against his own friends. Other pictures produced at about the same time are no less brutal than *White Heat*; for example, *Kiss of Death*, also portraying a manical murderer, has a scene in which Richard Widmark hurls a crippled old woman in a wheel chair down a flight of stairs to her death.

But the anti-social message of *White Heat* made an unforgettable impression upon me, because I saw it as an inmate of a federal prison, enjoying the Saturday night film-showing with my fellow prisoners. There are many decent, well-intentioned people in prison; many who recognize that the forces which drove them to vice or crime are inherent in our present social system. Related to this partial understanding is a deep bitterness, a feeling that the individual has no chance in a jungle society unless he adopts the ways of the jungle.

White Heat idealizes this code of the jungle, and advertises it as a "way of life." It made a strong impression on the prison inmates, especially on the younger men. There were long discussions after the showing: one could insist that Cagney is characterized as a madman in the picture. But Cagney is a famous actor. The prison audience—and that is probably true of other audiences—associated the fictitious character with Cagney's reputation. The spectators saw him as an attractive symbol of *toughness*, defending himself against a cruel and irrational society: "At least," it was said, "he has the guts to stand up and fight back!"

This emphasis on the individual's total depravity in a depraved society rejects the possibility of rational social cooperation. Man is doomed to prowl alone, a beast in the jungle.[13]

The debate over the pros and cons of *White Heat* has never really abated, and the literature referring to the film is extensive. *White Heat* is still integrated into many texts as indicative of this trend or that idea, depending on the concerns of the writers. For example, the celebrants of film noir, a term coined by French critics in the 1950s to denote (among other things) a film with an ambivalent moral outlook, point to *White Heat* as an exemplar of the ("devoid of social criticism") category.[14]

The violence in *White Heat* has obviously since been surpassed by many films, some of them doubtless inspired, unconsciously or otherwise, by Goff and Roberts's script. In retrospect, the possible detrimental influence of the film gives the screenwriters pause, since the pale imitations, surely, have had a perfidious social effect, even if they do simply reflect the growing integration of violence in modern society. "It was the story of a violent man," mused Roberts, "and you could hardly do it with-

13. John Howard Lawson, *Film in the Battle of Ideas* (New York: Masses and Mainstream, 1953), pp. 23–25.

14. See, especially, Paul Schrader, "Notes on *Film Noir*," *Film Comment* (Spring 1972), pp. 8–13, and Raymond Durgnat, "The Family Tree of *Film Noir*," *Cinema* (August 1970), pp. 49–56.

out the violence. The violence is part of his life, part of his nature. And in those days there wasn't as much concern about the violence. Of course, we were slightly concerned later on when we read a lot of the reviews and essays about the piece because it apparently had an enormous effect on people. Most of the reviews, remember, were excellent—we've never had reviews like that. But some of the essays were carping about the violence. Most of them, however, understood that it is hard to do a Greek tragedy without the tragedy."

Afterward

An amusing ancedote illustrates the ambivalence with which *White Heat* was greeted in some circles—for even the screenwriter's own mother had qualms about the movie. After *White Heat* was sneak-previewed at the Warner theater in Huntington Park, screenwriter Goff, flushed with pride and confident of a favorable audience reaction, asked his mother how she had liked it. She replied, "Well, of its type I suppose it's awfully good, but personally I prefer something like *The Philadelphia Story.*" Remembered Goff with a smile, "It was absolutely not her cup of tea."

Though honor has been accorded *White Heat* with the passage of time, it was bypassed for major awards in the year of its release, 1949, for it was really too controversial a selection. Only for Best Original Story was it nominated for an Academy Award; in that category, Virginia Kellogg lost to Douglas Morrow for *The Stratton Story.* Goff and Roberts went on to other things—to many other things. Among the movies they subsequently wrote (or co-wrote) together, apart from their off-and-on relationship with Cagney, are *Goodbye My Fancy* (1951), *Captain Horatio Hornblower* (1951), *O. Henry's Full House* (1952), *White Witch Doctor* (1953), *King of the Khyber Rifles* (1953), *Green Fire* (1954), *Serenade* (1956), *Band of Angels* (1957), *Midnight Lace* (1960), and *Legend of the Lone Ranger* (1981). Fed up with studios and producers who trampled on the niceties of their work, they turned to television in the early sixties, creating "The Rogues," writing episodes of "Mannix" for seven years, originating "Charlie's Angels," and producing "Nero Wolfe," among other credits. Since their first tandem effort they have not written except as a team, and as a team for roughly forty years they hold something of a record for longevity. Like most screenwriters, they have not cultivated publicity. But as of this writing, they are alive and well, their typewriters humming with imagination, in Hollywood.

I would like to acknowledge the assistance of Jean Frissell in the final preparation of this manuscript.

1. *Opening scene: The mail train heist.*

2. *The first motif of "white heat."*

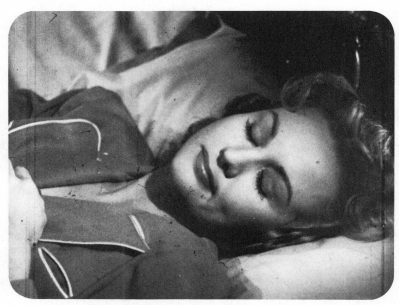

3. *"Verna's philosophy is simple: What's in it for Verna?"*

4. *Ma Jarrett (Margaret Wycherly) and Verna (Virginia Mayo).*

5. *Cody Jarrett's (James Cagney) blinding headache.*

6. *Sitting on the lap of Ma.*

7. *Treasury agent Philip Evans (John Archer).*

8. *"Ya like strawberries, don't ya?"*

9. "Where Ma goes, Cody goes . . . "

10. "I've been promised a vacation, you remember?"

41

11. *Hank Fallon (Edmond O'Brien) and Cody Jarrett in court.*

12. *"I guess his eyes ain't so good after solitary."*

13. Ma Jarrett assumes leadership of the gang.

14. Verna conspires with Big Ed Somers (Steve Cochran).

43

15. Ma Jarrett visits Cody in prison.

16. Portent of things to come.

44

17. *Surrogate Ma: Fallon rubs away Cody's headache.*

18. *"I got business on the outside."*

19. A visit from Fallon's "wife" (Fern Eggen).

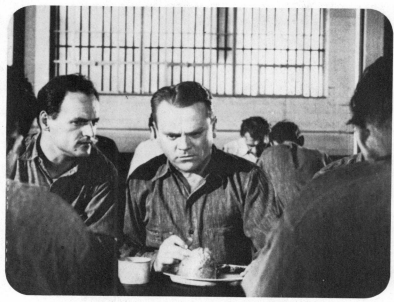

20. In the mess hall, Cody learns of Ma's death.

21. Cody goes berserk.

22. The convicts are stunned, as Cody is dragged away.

23. *"Oh, stuffy, huh? I'll give yuh a little air."*

24. *"Now tell me you're glad to see me, only say it low."*

25. The violent demise of Big Ed.

26. Rendezvous with the Trader (Fred Clark).

27. "Maybe I am nuts."

28. "Here's to us. 'Top of the world!'"

29. The Jarrett gang inside "the Trojan horse."

30. The ABC method of police surveillance.

31. *The oil refinery payroll robbery.*

32. *Bo Creel (Ian MacDonald) recognizes Fallon.*

33. *"Mother earth in metal."*

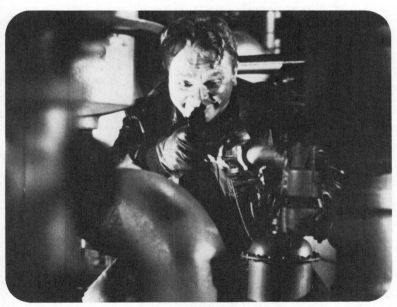

34. Surrounded.

53

35. "What's holding him up?"

36. "I made it, Ma! Top of the world!"

White Heat

Screenplay
by
IVAN GOFF
and
BEN ROBERTS

White Heat

FADE IN

Credits superimposed over panning dawn shot of mountainous terrain, bleak, ominous. On last credit camera reaches a sign which reads California State Line. As last credit fades out, pan up to show glistening steel ribbons of a railroad track as a train—modern but not diesel—approaches camera, thunders past.

LAP DISSOLVE TO:

1. INT. PASSENGER COACH   DAWN

Most of the occupants asleep. Big Ed Somers, leaning back in his seat, pushes his hat brim back, glances at his watch, then looks across aisle.

2. CLOSE SHOT   HAPPY TAYLOR

Moon-faced, sad-looking, Happy catches Big Ed's glance, looks at his own watch, nods to Big Ed.

3. EXT. RAILROAD TRACKS   LONG SHOT   DAWN

Train going through railroad cut. Pan to adjacent highway. A car is seen speeding along in the same direction as the train, moving past it.

LAP DISSOLVE TO:

4. INT. CODY JARRETT'S CAR   (PROCESS)   DAWN

Het Kohler is driving. Beside him sits Cody Jarrett, cold-eyed, merciless. Zuckie Hommel and Cotton Valetti sit in rear of car. Zuckie is garrulous; Cotton has a sallow, weak face. Cody looks at his watch, nudges Het, gestures for him to drive faster.

5.   EXT. HIGHWAY   MED. LONG SHOT   DAWN
Car picks up speed.

LAP DISSOLVE TO:

6.   EXT. MOUNTAINOUS TERRAIN   RAILROAD TRACKS   DAWN
as train approaches camera, starting its climb.

7.   CLOSE   RUNBY
on train wheels, slowing as train begins ascent.

8.   LONG SHOT   REAR ANGLE
as train disappears into the night, climbing mountain-
side.

9.   EXT. HIGHWAY   LONG SHOT   DAWN
Cody's car speeding along highway. Car swerves off
highway onto dirt road, jounces along rutted road.

LAP DISSOLVE TO:

10.   EXT. RAILROAD   NEAR TUNNEL MOUTH   DAWN
Cody's car comes across a small bridge, is braked to a
stop. The four men come swiftly from the car. Het and
Cotton carry sticks of dynamite, rolls of fuse wire, a detonating machine. They scurry down to the roadbed
where a spur forks off the main tracks.

11.   GROUP

CODY:
    Het—Cotton—the minute we got the train on the
    spur—start hoppin'. Zuckie—ya know what to do?

ZUCKIE:
    Sure, Cody. I throw the switch—then I beat it back
    to the—

CODY:
    Just do it. Don't gab so much.

Cody exits shot toward tunnel mouth. While Het pre-
pares his blasting equipment and Cotton checks his gun,

Zuckie tries to throw the switch. It is locked. Zuckie draws his gun, explodes the lock, throws switch.

11A.   CODY   AT TUNNEL MOUTH
He clambers up the side of the ravine, inches across to a ledge overlooking the tracks.

                                        LAP DISSOLVE TO:

12.   EXT. MOUNTAINOUS TERRAIN   DAWN
Train labors up a steep grade.

13.   INT. TRAIN   CLOSE   HAPPY TAYLOR
He looks at his watch, rises, starts for the rear of the train, passing Big Ed Somers, who feigns sleep.

                                        WIPE TO:

14.   INT. REAR COACH OF TRAIN   MED.   BRAKEMAN
He has just poured himself a cup of coffee from a thermos flask when Happy Taylor enters silently. The brakeman backs away from the muzzle of a revolver.

15.   EXT. LEDGE   AT MOUTH OF TUNNEL   CLOSE   NIGHT
on Cody, crouched tensely, waiting. In distance train whistle is heard.

16.   INT. REAR COACH OF TRAIN
The door to the coach is opened, arousing a moment's hope in the brakeman. Then Big Ed Somers enters, dragging the unconscious conductor, who has blood on his forehead. Big Ed has his revolver drawn.

BIG ED:
    The conductor didn't want to play. (Drops him to floor.) How's this guy?

HAPPY:
    Nice willin' guy.

BRAKEMAN (moistens lips):
    What do you want me to do?

BIG ED:
> Stop the train and let us off.

Brakeman reaches for emergency cord.

HAPPY:
> When we tell ya.

17.   EXT. TRAIN   DAWN
as it disappears into tunnel.

18.   INT. REAR COACH
Big Ed is looking out of the window. When the rear coach
enters the tunnel:

BIG ED (to brakeman):
> This is where we want off.

In desperation the brakeman dives for thermos flask and
swings it against Happy's skull, knocking him down.
Big Ed, pausing only long enough to shoot the brakeman, leaps across the caboose and pulls the emergency
cord, twice. Happy begins to get to his feet.

19.   EXT. TUNNEL MOUTH   HIGH ANGLE   SHOOTING PAST CODY
The engine appears, its brakes grinding. Cody leaps from
the ledge to the engine tender, gun drawn, and is in the
engine cab before the men know it.

20.   INT. ENGINE CAB
The engineer and fireman turn from their controls, stare
into the menace of Cody's gun. Their hands go up. The
train has stopped.

CODY:
> Get away from those controls. (Zuckie, who clam-
> bers aboard, takes the controls.)

FIREMAN:
> What's the idea?

CODY:
> You're seven minutes late. We decided to put on a new engineer.

ZUCKIE (as train starts slowly):
> Lot fancier'n my old coal-burner on the C and O.

CODY:
> Shut up!

21.   FULL SHOT
The engine veers off the main tracks onto the spur. Leaning from the cab, but keeping the engine crew covered, Cody shouts an order to Cotton and Het as they pass engine with equipment. They disappear toward mail car as train comes to a stop.

22.   EXT. AT REAR COACH
Big Ed Somers and Happy Taylor swing down, guns in hand, pelt up the adjacent track toward front of train.

23.   EXT. AT MAIL CAR
Cotton Valetti mounts the steps of the mail car, crashes the glass on top half of door, but does not disturb the protecting wire mesh.

COTTON:
> Open up and you won't get hurt.

For reply, a bullet from inside the mail car whizzes by his head. Cotton returns the fire, while Het Kohler ties a charge of dynamite to the door rail.

24.   CLOSE SHOT   HET KOHLER
Swiftly, with experienced fingers, he finishes tying the charge of dynamite to the door rail.

25.   MED.   IN ENGINE CAB
Cody's gun still menaces engine crew. Shots are heard.

ZUCKIE:
Sounds bad, Cody.

The exchange of looks between fireman and engineer at the name is not lost upon Cody, who snarls at Zuckie.

CODY:
Why don't ya give 'em my address, too?

25A.   EXT. MAIL CAR   HET, COTTON, BIG ED, AND HAPPY
retreat to a safe distance, camera panning. Het goes to blasting machine, pushes the plunger. There is a roar. The four men rush back into the smoke and fumes.

25B.   MED.   IN ENGINE CAB

CODY (yelling):
Don't fool around with the other bags! Just the Treasury stuff!

ENGINEER:
You won't get away with it, Cody.

CODY:
Cody, eh? (To Zuckie.) Go get the car started. (Coldly; to engineer.) You got a good memory for names. Too good. (He cocks his .45 as Zuckie starts to descend.)

26.   CLOSE   FIREMAN
his face fixed with horror. Cody's gun explodes off-screen, sending death into the body of the engineer. As he crumples, his arm trails lifelessly, without strength, along the fireman's sleeve, drops from sight. The fireman stares down, then back at Cody. In Cody's face he sees mirrored his own death, and is afraid.

FIREMAN:
I got a wife—kids . . . [1]

White Heat

27.   CLOSE SHOT   ZUCKIE
standing on railbed beside cab. He turns, listens, ashen-faced. Cody's gun spits death again.

28.   INT. ENGINE CAB
The fireman is in the act of falling. As he hits against the wall of instruments his arm strikes the blowoff cock lever, jerking it open. There is a roar of escaping steam, and, simultaneously, Zuckie's piercing scream.

29.   CLOSE   ZUCKIE
The full force of the engine's steam pressure erupts in his face—scalding, blinding, shooting a hundred feet past him. Zuckie's scream lasts but a second, then becomes a piteous moan as he falls.

30.   INT. ENGINE CAB
With his foot, Cody kicks up the blowoff cock. The steam instantly subsiding, he descends from the cab.

31.   EXT. ENGINE
As Cody reaches the ground, with hardly a glance for the writhing Zuckie, the other bandits run into shot. Het Kohler triumphantly holds up a registered-mail bag. Cody takes it, with a look of satisfaction. Cotton bends over his pal Zuckie, drags him up.

CODY (savagely):
Let's get out of here!

He starts for the car, followed by Big Ed, Het Kohler with the detonating machine, and Happy Taylor, lending Cotton Valetti a hand in carrying Zuckie. Behind them all is death and destruction.

DISSOLVE TO:

32.   INT. BROADCASTING BOOTH   CLOSE ON ANNOUNCER   DAY

RADIO ANNOUNCER (into microphone):
A week has passed since bandits jumped a mail train

coming out of the High Sierra tunnel and fled with
three hundred thousand dollars in federal currency,
leaving four dead. Treasury authorities now believe
. . .

WIPE TO:

33.   INT. MOUNTAIN SHED   DAY

Two cars inside shed. At one of them, listening to the
radio, stands Cotton. Also listening, while he stands
guard leaning against entrance to shed, is Big Ed, rifle
held in gloved hands. They are both bundled up against
the cold. We hear the scream of strong winds. In background is a rustic cabin. Its door opens and Het and
Happy, heavily bundled, come out, leaning against the
wind.

RADIO ANNOUNCER'S VOICE:
. . . that the gang has escaped to Arizona, where
today a bank was raided and two tellers killed with
the same cold-bloodedness that characterized the
tunnel robbery.

COTTON (snaps off radio):
Now we're supposed to be in Arizona.

BIG ED:
Any place'd be better than this.

Cotton joins him at door as their "relief" arrives. Big Ed
hands Het the rifle and starts back to cabin with Cotton.

34.   EXT. DOLLY SHOT   BIG ED AND COTTON

BIG ED:
We gotta blow out of here.

COTTON:
Cody calls chargin' roadblocks unscientific.

BIG ED:
It ain't safe to have a crackpot givin' orders. About
time somebody took over.

64

COTTON:
> Who, for instance?

BIG ED:
> A good friend of mine. Me.

COTTON:
> Where d'ya want the body sent?

Big Ed glares at him as they enter cabin.

35. INT. MOUNTAIN CABIN
A table, wooden chairs, a couch, an unlit fireplace. Cody sits in a chair near bedroom door, cleaning his .45, a yard from Ma Jarrett, who is cooking stew on a small two-burner oil stove. The founders of Mother's Day would have reconsidered it quickly if they had ever met Ma, a woman in her middle sixties. Cotton and Big Ed enter. Cotton goes to a couch on which sprawls the moaning Zuckie, face bandaged. Everyone is bundled up against the cold.

CODY:
> Been playing golf, Ed?

BIG ED:
> We got a sackful of dough and we're holed up like a bunch of gophers. When are we movin' outa here?

CODY:
> Maybe tomorrow—maybe 1952. I'll mull it over. All right? (Their eyes meet. Ed gives way, mouth tightening. Cody grins, goes to the stove, sniffs appreciatively.) Smells good, Ma.[2]

MA JARRETT:
> If you're gettin' hungry I could use some help, Son.

CODY (kicks bedroom door):
> Hey, Verna!

VERNA'S VOICE:
> Yeah, Cody . . . Comin'.

White Heat

36.   INT. BEDROOM   MED. SHOT   VERNA JARRETT

Verna moves from the bed toward door, tightening her robe. Her face is beautiful, and about as warm as snow. Verna's philosophy is simple: What's in it for Verna?[3]

37.   INT. CABIN

MA JARRETT (as Verna enters):
   If it ain't the Sleepin' Beauty!

VERNA (snapping):
   What else does a girl do around this palais de dance?[4]

MA JARRETT:
   There's plenty ya can do besides wearin' out the mattress.

VERNA:
   It's the only place I don't freeze. (Appeals to Cody.) I been cold for a week, Cody. Not even a fire. Who's gonna see a little bit of smoke a hundred miles from nowhere?

CODY:
   Help Ma with the grub.

Verna shrugs, moves to stove. Zuckie moans.

CODY (to Cotton):
   How's he doin'?

COTTON:
   He's gettin' worse, Cody. He needs a doc.

CODY:
   When the time comes.

VERNA:
   Ya want some coffee, Ed?

Big Ed looks at her, his passion but thinly disguised. Cody looks from one to the other swiftly.

66

BIG ED:
> Thanks, Verna!

CODY (sharply):
> Let him get his own! My wife don't wait on nobody.

Big Ed seems about to say something, thinks better of it, moves over to stove to pour his own coffee.

38.   CLOSE ON CODY   (SITS IN CHAIR, BEGINS TO LOAD HIS .45)

CODY:
> Ya know somethin', Verna? If I turned my back long enough for Big Ed to put a hole in it—there'd be a hole in it. (Chuckles.) Big Ed. Know why they call him that? 'Cause his ideas are big. Well, one day he'll get a really big idea—and that'll be his last. (He frowns suddenly, shakes his head as if in pain.)

39.   CLOSE   MA JARRETT
watching Cody closely, with concern.

40.   CLOSE   ON CODY
Recovering momentarily, he goes to place another bullet in revolver chamber, but his fingers seem to lose control and the bullet, missing its goal, drops to floor. Cody frowns, stares glassily. The pain returns. An agonized groan escapes him. He rises blindly, stumbles into the bedroom.

41.   MED. FULL SHOT
The others have watched Cody's exit silently. Ma Jarrett is genuinely alarmed. With a glare at the others, she follows Cody into bedroom. The door closes.

42.   INT. BEDROOM
Ma Jarrett bolts door. Cody has flung himself across bed. He breathes laboredly—sweating—his fingers clutch-

ing the rough blanket. Ma goes to window, pulls down the blinds, then moves swiftly over to Cody. She clutches his hand tightly, rubs his back, croons over him—the tigress suddenly becomes gentle with her cub.

CODY (with difficulty):
    Ma!

MA JARRETT:
    I'm here, Cody.

43.   INT. CABIN   CLOSE   VERNA AND BIG ED

VERNA (trembling; a whisper):
    That's the second one in a month.

BIG ED (thinly):
    He's nuts. Just like his old man.

Verna looks at him speculatively.

44.   INT. BEDROOM
    Under Ma's ministrations, Cody is regaining control.

MA JARRETT:
    It's these mountains, Cody. It's no good for you. Cold all the time. The air's hard to breathe. Let's get out, Son.

CODY:
    I'm all right now.

MA JARRETT:
    Is it goin'? Are you sure?

CODY:
    Yeah . . . (Shakes head.) Like havin' a buzz saw inside my head. (Starts to rise.)

MA JARRETT:
    Not yet, Cody. Don't let 'em see you like this. Might give some of 'em ideas.

CODY:
Always worryin' about Cody.

He sits back on bed. While Ma pours him drink he rubs away the last traces of pain. Ma hands him drink.

MA JARRETT:
Top of the world, Son.

CODY:
Don't know what I'd do without ya, Ma. (Downs drink.)

MA JARRETT:
Better? (Cody nods.) Now, go out there and show 'em you're all right.

Cody pats her hand, exits into outer room.[5]

45. INT. CABIN
The others look at Cody as he comes out of bedroom.

CODY:
What're ya all gapin' at? (To Verna.) I told you to help with the groceries.

As Verna turns back to stove, we hear Happy calling "Cody!" off-screen. Then, excited, he runs in from outside.

HAPPY:
Hey, Cody! There's a storm comin'. Every road'll be blocked, the guy said.

CODY:
What guy?

HAPPY:
On the radio.

CODY:
How long did he give it?

HAPPY:
> Tonight.

CODY:
> That's what I been waitin' for. Start packin'.

MA JARRETT:
> Are ya sure it's safe, Cody?

CODY:
> A storm keeps everybody busy. (Designating jobs.) Chains on all the tires. Clean it good in here. Don't leave any calling cards. (Goes to Happy, cuffs him hard.) I told ya to keep away from the radio. If that battery's dead, it'll have company.

> DISSOLVE TO:

46.   INT. BEDROOM CLOSE BED
A suitcase is dropped onto the bed. Cody's hands open the lid to check on the contents—stack upon stack of new twenty-dollar bills. When the lid is closed again, it bears Verna's shadow.

VERNA'S VOICE (a purr):
> It's your suitcase, Cody. Why don't ya keep it all?

Draw back to show Cody looking at her, sardonically. Dressed now, she wears a fur coat.

CODY:
> You're cute. Come here.

VERNA (as he fondles her):
> Why don't ya? We could travel, buy things. That's what money's for. I'd look good in a mink coat, honey.

CODY:
> You'd look good in a shower curtain. (He kisses her.)

47.   INT. MOUNTAIN CABIN
It is stripped bare. Cotton Valetti and Ma Jarrett are filling a sack with all the dishes and the pots and empty

bottles. Zuckie lies on the couch, too weak now to move. The preparations of the last half hour have worked up an enormous fear within him.

ZUCKIE:
Cotton! . . . Cotton!

COTTON (crossing to him):
Yeah, Zuckie. I'm here.

ZUCKIE:
We're pals, Cotton. You'll see I get away all right? See I get to a doc?

COTTON (uncertainly):
Sure, Zuckie. Sure.

Cody comes in from bedroom, followed by Verna. They are bundled up for outdoors. Cody carries the suitcase.

MA JARRETT:
Everything's set.

ZUCKIE:
Cody . . .?

CODY:
Yeah.

ZUCKIE:
I was pretty good back there on the train, huh, Cody? Pretty good for my first job, huh?

CODY:
You were great.

ZUCKIE (hopefully):
Ya won't leave me here? Ya'll take me with ya?

CODY:
Can't take a chance bein' stopped with you in the car, Zuckie. I'll send a doc back right away.

The others look at Cody. They all know he is lying. So does Zuckie. He fumbles blindly for the gun beneath his pillow. It is gone. Ma Jarrett shows it to Cody. With a helpless cry, Zuckie collapses back on pillow.

ZUCKIE:
> You're gonna let me die! If I had my eyes . . . If I had my eyes . . .

Cody leads the others out, Cotton looking back conscience-stricken at his pal.

48.   EXT. CABIN
Zuckie's moaning can be heard as group comes out. Cotton lingers, agonized.

ZUCKIE'S VOICE:
> Cody! . . . Cody! . . . *Cotton!*

MA JARRETT:
> What if they find him, Cody? You know how Zuckie talks.

CODY:
> He won't be talkin' . . . Cotton!

They have reached the cars, which Het and Big Ed have moved out into the open. Cotton runs up.

COTTON:
> Ya meant what you said, Cody? About sendin' a doc?

CODY:
> A specialist. You. (Hands him revolver.) You're such a pal, make it easy for him. (Cotton stares at revolver.) Step on it. (The others watch tensely. Cotton wavers a second, then moves slowly toward cabin.) We're three hundred miles from the tunnel, Ma, so what've they got? A corpse without a record. Nothin' to tie him in with the tunnel job—or with us.

49.   EXT. ANOTHER ANGLE   (SHOOTING PAST GROUP TOWARD
        CABIN)
        as Cotton enters cabin. The pause is almost endless. In-
        tercut close reaction shots: Het and Happy, tense; Cody
        and Ma, impassive; Big Ed and Verna, exchanging looks.
        Then the revolver shot from inside cabin.

50.   INT. CABIN
        Cotton, bent over Zuckie, has just fired at the ceiling.

        COTTON (low; swift):
            Don't make a sound, Zuckie. I'll try to come back.
            Here's some smokes. (Slips pack of cigarettes into
            Zuckie's pocket, exits.)

        ZUCKIE:
            Thanks, Cotton . . . Thanks.

51.   EXT. GROUP
        As Cotton comes out, face grim, moves toward cars.

        CODY:
            We'll separate. Het, you take the second car. Go east
            when ya hit the highway. Double back over the
            bridge. And stay on the dirt roads.

        Cody gets behind the wheel of the first sedan as the
        others pile into the cars. As Cotton reaches Cody's car
        and gets in, he gives Cody a peculiarly triumphant look,
        unnoticed by Cody. The first car starts down along the
        narrow road, the second car following. Camera pans until
        they round a bend in the road.

52.   EXT. FRONT DOOR OF CABIN
        It opens slowly. Zuckie stumbles out.

        ZUCKIE:
            No, Cotton—I don't trust ya—I don't trust no-
            body—ya won't come back—ya won't come back . . .

53. EXT. HIGH ANGLE SHOT   ZUCKIE

as he gropes his way into the clearing with his last remaining strength. He falls, rises, lurches forward. A tree is in his path. He collides with it, falls. He tries to rise, but his strength fails and he sprawls unconscious.[6]

SLOW DISSOLVE TO:

54. INT. MORGUE   CLOSE SHOT ON SHEET   DAY

held up by a man's hand so that it momentarily obscures everything. A flashbulb explodes. Then as chief of police's voice is heard, the sheet is lowered back onto Zuckie's body which (not until covered) is revealed on slab.

CHIEF'S VOICE:
Hope I didn't get you up here on a wild-goose chase, Mr. Evans.

EVANS'S VOICE:
The geese we're looking for are pretty wild.

Visible now, flanking body, are the police surgeon and Philip Evans, a tall, lean Treasury agent; the chief of police behind Evans; and Ernie Trent, a bespectacled, studious-looking technician removing spent flashbulb from his camera.

CHIEF OF POLICE:
Couple of hunters found him frozen up in the mountains and we started wondering. A stranger— bullet hole in the roof of the cabin—and particularly the condition of his face. Tell him, Doc.

POLICE SURGEON:
Despite the third-degree burn the eyebrows and hairline weren't even singed. That means either boiling water or steam.

CHIEF OF POLICE:
So we thought of a steam engine.

74

EVANS:

> Good hunch. Let me have his clothes. Ernie, get his fingerprints and take a mask of his face.

CHIEF OF POLICE:

> Here you are, Mr. Evans. Nothing in the pockets except this pack of cigarettes.

From a wall the chief has taken a hanger supporting Zuckie's clothes. As he hands it to Evans, move in close to show pack of cigarettes pinned to clothes in cellophane envelope.

DISSOLVE TO:

55. INT. EVANS'S OFFICE   NIGHT

Close on Willie Rolph, a weasellike informer.

WILLIE:

> . . . So, like ya told me, Mr. Evans, I made the rounds for a month—driftin' kinda—not too eager—you know, just droppin' a word in the right ears that I'm interested in pickin' up a few hot dollars. But not a buck from the tunnel job showed up.

Through this, pull back to show Evans at his desk. His office is furnished with steel files, a teletype; on the wall behind him, between crossed flags, is a picture of the president.[7]

EVANS:

> They haven't buried it in tin cans, Willie. Keep looking.

WILLIE:

> I'll go out the back way if you don't mind. Any o' the boys spotted me comin' up here, I'll be in a real jam. (He backs out, almost upsetting Ernie Trent, who enters from the lab, carrying two photographs.)

TRENT:
Get anything out of Willie?

EVANS:
A blank.

TRENT:
This'll cheer you up, Phil. (Hands him photo.) Spectrograph of some dirt from the tunnel. (Hands him second photo.) Spectrograph of dust deposits from the dead man's clothes.

56.   INSERT   PHOTOGRAPHS OF SPECTROSCOPE FINDINGS
The enlargements of the dust particles in each photograph are seen to match exactly.

TRENT'S VOICE:
No doubt about it. Identical. All adds up and places our friend in the morgue right smack at the scene of the crime.

57.   BACK TO SCENE
Evans returns photos to Ernie with grim satisfaction.

EVANS:
Looks like we're in business. (Teletype starts. Evans moves to it eagerly, reads heading.) From Washington . . . (slowly.) Have—no—fingerprint—record—dead—man . . . (Teletype pauses; glumly.) That's one I never expected. Dead man. Dead end. (Teletype resumes; reads slowly but with mounting excitement.) But—prints—on—cellophane—of—cigarette—package—belong—Giovanni—Cotton—Valetti—known—member—Jarrett—gang . . . (Picks up Zuckie's death mask.) I thought you were never going to talk . . .

DISSOLVE TO

58.   EXT. AUTO COURT   SIGN   NIGHT
reading: Milbanke Motels—All Over Los Angeles. Pan

down as a dark coupe drives in entrance, skirts around the back line of auto courts, stops.

59. EXT. AT COUPE
Cody gets out, looks around quickly, goes to rear of a darkened auto court, raps softly on door, calls "Ma" in a low voice. No answer. Cody frowns, moves quickly to adjoining auto court, enters.

60. INT. AUTO COURT   NIGHT
Verna is at a mirror admiring herself in her new mink coat as Cody comes in.

CODY (tensely):
Where's Ma?

VERNA:
She went to the market.

CODY:
Which one?

VERNA:
Ma don't tell me those little details. What difference does it make, which one?

CODY:
The difference is they got Zuckie in a morgue upstate. The T-men tied him in with us on the tunnel job.

VERNA (startled):
What?

CODY:
Dunno how they did it. Somebody musta tipped them. (Looks impatiently at watch.)

VERNA:
It's always somebody tipped them . . . Never the cops are smart.

77

CODY (more tensely):
>   We got enough food for a week! What she have to
>   go out for?

VERNA (sardonically):
>   Ya like strawberries, don't ya? Well, she just *had* to
>   get some for her boy.

Cody gives her a look.

DISSOLVE TO:

61.   MARKET   CLOSE ON MA JARRETT   NIGHT
She picks up a box of strawberries from the sidewalk
display and goes inside to make other purchases. Pan
to a nearby telephone booth.

62.   INT. TELEPHONE BOOTH   NIGHT

GOVERNMENT AGENT (into phone):
>   . . . Her car's parked outside pointing north. Forty-
>   one black De Soto sedan—California eight-L-nine-
>   four-nine-four—forty-nine tabs. There'll be a marker
>   on the rear bumper . . . That what I thought, Mr.
>   Evans. Where Cody goes, Ma goes. (Hangs up, tears
>   handkerchief in two.)

63.   EXT. STREET   GOVERNMENT AGENT
comes out of phone booth, walks along sidewalk to Ma's
sedan, pretends to tie shoelace on rear bumper, hangs
a small strip of handkerchief from guard, innocently
crosses street out of shot.

DISSOLVE TO:

64.   INT. EVANS'S CAR   (PROCESS)   NIGHT
An inconspicuous dark business coupe. Evans marks a
street map on his lap. A second agent drives.

DISSOLVE TO:

65.   STREET   INSIDE EVANS'S CAR   NIGHT
parked at the curb, sixty feet behind Ma's sedan.

EVANS (into microphone):
> We'll use the ABC method. I'm B. I'll keep first po-
> sition behind suspect on Orengo Boulevard.

66.   INSERT   MAP OF LOS ANGELES ON EVANS'S LAP
his pencil marking ABC on the appropriate street locations.

67.   INT. A SMALL SEDAN   PARKED IN DIFFERENT STREET
LOCATION
The agent listens intently as Evans's voice comes over.

EVANS'S VOICE:
> Two two seven, you're A. You drive parallel on Lat-
> imer.

AGENT (into mike):
> Okay.

68.   INT. ANOTHER SMALL SEDAN   EXT. ANOTHER STREET
as another agent listens intently.

EVANS'S VOICE:
> Three two three, you're C. The same on Fairchild.
> Got that?

AGENT (into mike):
> Okay.

69.   AT EVANS'S CAR   (SHOOTING TOWARD MARKET)
Evans reacts to something he sees off-screen.[8]

70.   MARKET   MA JARRETT   (FROM EVANS'S ANGLE)
as she exits, moving to her car. She carries a full bag of
purchases.

71.   EXT. STREET   HIGH ANGLE   LONG SHOT
Ma Jarrett's car pulls away from curb. Evans's car follows, keeping a fair distance between them.

72.   INT. EVANS'S CAR   (PROCESS)

    EVANS (into microphone):
        Suspect proceeding dead ahead on Beverly, Approaching Alvarado.

73.   INT. MA JARRETT'S CAR   (PROCESS)
    Her sixth sense makes her glance into rearview mirror.

74.   THROUGH REARVIEW MIRROR   MA JARRETT'S
    ANGLE   (PROCESS)
    She sees Evans's car, some distance behind.

75.   INT. MA JARRETT'S CAR   (PROCESS)
    She frowns. As car reaches corner she turns sharply.

76.   EXT. INTERSECTION   MA JARRETT'S CAR
    as it makes the turn.

77.   INT. MA JARRETT'S CAR   (PROCESS)
    Again Ma glances into rearview mirror.

78.   THROUGH REARVIEW MIRROR   MA JARRETT'S ANGLE
    (PROCESS)
    Evans's car is seen as it reaches the intersection, proceeds directly ahead without turning.

79.   INT. MA JARRETT'S CAR   (PROCESS)
    Her mouth relaxes a little.

80.   INT. EVANS'S CAR   (PROCESS)

    EVANS (into microphone):
        Suspect turned south on Alvarado . . . A, pick her up at Second. We'll take your position.

81.   EXT. STREET   HIGH ANGLE
    As Ma Jarrett's car moves across another intersection, still going south, a small dark sedan makes the turn from

the cross street and takes up its position behind her car, keeping a discreet distance.

82.   INT. CAR A   (PROCESS)

OPERATIVE (into microphone):
   Got her. Traveling dead ahead on Alvarado. Twenty miles an hour.

83.   INT. MA JARRETT'S CAR   (PROCESS)
Ma, tough to convince, still feels eyes upon her. Looks glancingly in rearview mirror again, shakes head slightly, then looks front, swings wheel.

84.   INT. CAR A   (SHOOTING FROM BEHIND OPERATIVE) (PROCESS)

OPERATIVE (into microphone):
   Suspect turning east on Third.

85.   INT. EVANS'S CAR   (PROCESS)

EVANS (into microphone):
   Let her go. C, cut in fast and pick her up.

86.   INT. MA JARRETT'S CAR   (PROCESS)
This time when she looks into the rearview mirror and sees the road clear behind her, she grins, satisfied that she has thrown any pursuer off her trail.

87.   EXT. SIDE STREET
As Ma Jarrett's car comes past, Car C—a small gun-metal sedan—turns in from the side street and takes its position behind Ma's car at a discreet interval.

88.   INT. CAR C   (PROCESS)

OPERATIVE (into microphone):
   Got her. Going due east. About thirty . . . Hold the phone! She's turning left on Baxter.

89.   INT. EVANS'S CAR   (PROCESS)

EVANS (into microphone):
   I'll cut in and pick her up as she comes through. C,
   turn off and parallel Baxter.

Evans's car turns swiftly into a cross street.

90.   MA JARRETT'S CAR
It proceeds along Baxter past a corner, where Evans's
car cuts in behind her.

91.   INT. EVANS'S CAR   (SHOOTING THROUGH WINDSHIELD)
Ma's car not far ahead. Suddenly a truck backs out from
a building, right in the path of Evans's car, which avoids
an accident only by wheeling over to curb.

EVANS:
   Get around it!

Evans's driver backs, wheels around the obstructing
truck. But the street is empty. A few yards away is a
turnoff.

EVANS (into microphone):
   A, C—cut into Baxter again! I've lost her! (Indicating turnoff.) Down there.

The car makes the turn.

                                          WIPE TO:

92.   INT. EVANS'S CAR   (PROCESS)   NIGHT
as it cruises. Evans's face tells the whole story.

EVANS (into microphone):
   Come in A. Any trace? (A harsh crackling.) Come
   in C. Come in C. (Crackling persists.)

EVANS'S DRIVER:
   Dead spot, Phil.

EVANS:
   It would be. Turn around. We'll go back.

93. EXT. STREET   NEAR MILBANKE MOTELS   PANNING
     Evans's driver backs into driveway of auto court, pre-
     paratory to making turn. Evans glances out of window.
     Camera holds as car stops and driver puts it into first
     gear. Evans grips driver's arm.

94. MA JARRETT'S CAR   (EVANS'S ANGLE)
     Parked before one of the rear bungalows. Camera dol-
     lies up swiftly to close on the strip of telltale handker-
     chief affixed to the rear bumper.

95. INT. EVANS'S CAR
     Evans, tense with excitement, furiously tries the radio
     controls, but they are still in the dead spot.

     EVANS (opening car door):
         Beat it up the hill—call the others.

     DRIVER:
         You're not going to tackle them alone?

     EVANS:
         I'll just keep an eye on 'em. Hurry. (As the car drives
         off Evans heads for rear of auto court, gun in hand.)

96. INT. AUTO COURT—CODY, VERNA, MA   NIGHT
     They are finishing packing with the dexterity of people
     who do it often and swiftly. The atmosphere is tense.

     VERNA:
         What's the use of money if we gotta start runnin'
         every time somebody sees a shadow?

     MA JARRETT:
         It was only a feelin' I had, Cody. I could've been
         wrong.

     CODY:
         Your hunches are never wrong, Ma. We leave the
         sedan. That's the one they'll be lookin' for. Get the

bags. I'll back up the coupe. (He exits through back door.)

97.   EXT. REAR OF AUTO COURT
Pan Cody from the rear of auto court to his parked car. He slides behind the wheel.

98.   MED. CLOSE   CODY
As he leans forward and inserts the key in the ignition lock, the figure of Phil Evans materializes out of the darkness and levels a revolver at Cody's head.

EVANS:
You're not going anywhere, Jarrett. Get your hands up where I can see them.

It might be a smile that Cody directs at Evans, but the moon is playing tricks with light and shade. He raises his hands.

99.   INT. CODY'S CAR   CLOSE AT TOP OF WINDSHIELD
Cody's hands in shot. Attached to driver's sun visor is a .45, only inches from Cody's upraised hands.

100.   EVANS AND CODY
Evans reaches his free hand forward, snaps down the door handle, opens door. The enigmatic look remains on Cody's face as he twists his body and swings feet out, hands still upraised. Evans watches intently. Cody isn't the surrendering type.

101.   CODY   (EVANS'S ANGLE)
With a flashing movement of his arm, Cody acts. He fires practically at the same instant that he grabs his gun, falling away as he shoots.

102.   CLOSE   EVANS
The bullet in his right shoulder spins him around. He

clutches wound in a paroxysm of pain, tries to lift gun, but it drops limply from his hand as he falls.

103.   FULL SHOT
As Ma Jarrett and Verna rush to join Cody in the car, voices come over—disturbed auto-court patrons, a woman's shrill cry. The car roars away.

104.   EXT. FRONT OF MOTOR COURT
Cody's car swerves onto the road, brakes screeching.

105.   EVANS'S CAR   TOP OF HILL
Driver sees Cody's car, reacts, puts car in gear, speeds down toward auto court.

106.   EXT. FRONT OF MOTOR COURT
Cody's car, making turn onto road, veers crazily for an instant, is righted, speeds off.

107.   EVANS'S CAR
As it speeds down road from opposite direction.

108.   EXT. MOTOR COURT
As Evans's car draws level with court, slowing down, a group is seen emerging from rear of auto court, among them the injured Evans, supported by two auto-court patrons. Evans gestures to driver to follow escaping car. The siren is heard as Evans's car takes off in pursuit.

                                                  WIPE TO:

109.   EXT. STREET   CODY'S CAR
as it speeds down street toward corner.

109A.   INT. CODY'S CAR   CODY, MA, VERNA   (PROCESS)
Cody, face grim, looks in rearvision mirror, sees nothing, steps down on accelerator.

109B.   EXT. STREET   CODY'S CAR
          as it makes swerving turn around corner.

109C.   EXT. STREET   AGENT'S CAR
          as it makes turn into street, comes racing down in direc-
          tion Cody's car has taken. Siren is heard.

109D.   FLASH SHOT   TRENT IN CAR   (PROCESS)
          as he steps down on accelerator. Siren heard over shot.

109E.   CODY'S CAR
          racing down street. Siren heard faintly in background.

109F.   INT. CODY'S CAR   CODY, MA, VERNA   (PROCESS)
          Cody and others react to sound of siren. Cody's eyes
          narrow. He looks ahead, gets his idea; a faint, humor-
          less smile touches his mouth. He starts to swing wheel.

110.   EXT. STREET
          Cody swings car sharply, turns onto the incline of a ramp.
          As car disappears up ramp, pan up to glittering sign of
          Drive-in Theater.

111.   EXT. STREET   SHOOTING TOWARD CORNER
          Siren screaming, the federal car wheels around corner,
          speeds down the street.

112.   MED. FULL   DRIVE-IN THEATER PAYBOOTH   NIGHT
          Cody gives the cashier the admission money.

          CASHIER (as siren screams):
             Happens every night. Ruins the movie.

          Cody douses car lights, drives through the entrance.
                                                   DISSOLVE TO:

113.   INSIDE DRIVE-IN THEATER   NIGHT
          A Warner Brothers picture (*Task Force*) is on the screen
          as Cody's car swings into position behind the massed

cars.[9] An attendant hands in the usual small loudspeaker, which is suspended in car over a side window.

114.   INT. CODY'S CAR
They sit tensely, rigidly. A vendor puts his head in the window on Ma's side.

VENDOR:
Popcorn? Candy?

MA JARRETT:
Beat it!

Blinking, the vendor retreats. Cody turns down the volume control so that the sound from screen is barely audible. The siren gradually recedes.

VERNA:
This is great, but where do we go after the second feature?

CODY:
I'm the only one goin' anyplace.

MA JARRETT:
Where, Cody?

CODY:
To give myself up.

MA JARRETT:
What are you talkin' about? You haven't a chance. Four dead—it'll be the gas chamber for sure.

CODY:
You don't think I'm dumb enough to turn my self over to the T-men, do ya?

VERNA:
What's the difference? The minute ya walk into the cops *they* turn you over.

CODY:
Ya remember Scratch Morton?

VERNA (as Ma thinks):
Little fella on the lam from Illinois? You and him had a talk one night.

CODY:
That's the one.

MA JARRETT:
I remember, Cody. Knocked over a hotel payroll in Springfield.

CODY:
Same night we were at the tunnel. Handy, huh?

MA JARRETT:
Talk plain, son. What's that got to do with it?

CODY:
I pulled that Springfield heist—not Scratch Morton. I'm goin' to Illinois and take a state rap. Most I'll get is two years.

VERNA:
And when ya get out they're still waitin' for ya for the tunnel job.

CODY:
What tunnel job? Why, the day those hoodlums were killin' innocent people on a train, I was pushin' in a hotel in Springfield. I couldn't be in both places at once, could I? Little plan I cooked up—before we pulled the tunnel job.

MA JARRETT:
Cody, you're the smartest there is.

VERNA:
Sure, it's smart. But what about me? What am I supposed to do for two years?

MA JARRETT:
The same as before he married you!

CODY:
Better not, honey. I'll be back.

VERNA (takes the hint):
I'll be waitin' for ya, Cody. You can trust me. (Kisses him.)

CODY:
If the T-men pick you up, you don't know anything. Haven't seen me for months. You do all the talkin', Ma.

MA JARRETT:
I can handle 'em.

CODY:
Verna—you cry a little—like you're sad. (Verna nods.)

MA JARRETT:
How're you gonna make it to Illinois?

CODY:
Private plane. Don't worry. I'll get there. (Gets out of car.) Goodbye, Ma. Be a break to get rid of me for a while, huh?

MA JARRETT:
If you ever need me, I'll be around.[10]

Cody grins, winks at her. He closes car door, surveys the area carefully, hitches his trousers, starts off.

DISSOLVE TO:

115. INT. EVANS'S OFFICE   FULL SHOT   DAY
Evans, arm in a sling, interrogates Ma Jarrett and Verna. With stoic heroism, Verna restrains her tears, sniffing into a lace handkerchief. In this scene, Ma is never at a loss, gives out with her best Sunday manner. Present

are the two federal agents who brought them in, Jim Donovan and Ted Clark.

MA JARRETT:

. . . I tell you I only wanted to cheer up Verna. She's been blue all these weeks—missing Cody so much. So I went to the market to buy things for a real spread. Thought it might make her feel better. That right, Verna? (Verna nods.)

EVANS:

Yet as soon as you returned to the auto court you left again. Why?

MA JARRETT:

We decided to go to a movie instead.

EVANS:

What theater?

MA JARRETT:

The Sun-Val Drive-In.

EVANS:

What picture?

MA JARRETT:

Task Force. Exciting. Verna liked it a lot.

EVANS:

Cody like it?

MA JARRETT:

How could he? I told you, Cody hasn't been in California for months.

EVANS:

I suppose he shot me all the way from another state?

MA JARRETT:

What makes you think it was Cody shot you? Lots of people have guns.

EVANS:
    I was as close to him as I am to you.

MA JARRETT:
    Anybody else see him?[11]

EVANS:
    Just you and his wife.

MA JARRETT:
    Oh. 'Course, being an old woman I don't know much about the law. But I hear you gotta have witnesses to make anything stand up in court. You see Cody last night, Verna? (Verna shakes her head.) Makes you the only one, Mr. Evans, doesn't it?

EVANS (wryly):
    It seems to. And if Cody's been out of California for months, I suppose he couldn't possibly have engineered that train robbery six weeks ago.

MA JARRETT:
    Train robbery! Mr. Evans, I don't have to sit and listen to you accuse my boy without any proof! Besides, I know my rights. You can't keep us here. You've got nothing on us.

EVANS:
    All right, Mrs. Jarrett. That'll be all for now.

MA JARRETT:
    That's better. Come on, Verna. Stop crying. Nobody's going to hurt you.

As they exit Ma Jarrett gives Evans a triumphant look. When the two women are gone, the men exchange wry glances.

                                            DISSOLVE TO:

115A.   INSERT   FRONT PAGE   SPRINGFIELD HERALD-NEWS
    Big headlines, accompanied by photo of Cody, proclaim:

White Heat

CODY JARRETT SURRENDERS
Confesses Robbery
Of Palace Hotel

DISSOLVE TO:

115B. INT. EVANS'S OFFICE MED. CLOSE ON EVANS
He is bending over the teletype as it taps out a message, then moves back to his desk, grimly delighted by what he has read. The intercom buzzes. Evans flips key open.

MISS BENSON'S VOICE:
Mr. Fallon just arrived from the airport.

EVANS:
Send him right in.

He comes around desk as door opens and Hank Fallon enters. He is clean-cut, lithe, good-humored. They shake hands.

FALLON:
Hello, Phil.

EVANS:
Good to see you again, Hank. You're looking great.

FALLON:
It's that prison diet. Great chef in San Quentin. Best assignment I ever had. I hated to leave.

EVANS (grins):
I can imagine. Anyway, you did a whale of a job.

FALLON:
Most talkative little con I ever shared a cell with. And the last, I hope. (Eagerly, as Evans doesn't react.) How about it, Phil?[12] Look at me. College degree, lovable personality—and I spend most of my time in prison, an undercover specialist. Eight sentences in five years! I joined the Treasury Department to put criminals behind bars—and here *I* am, stir crazy!

92

EVANS (inwardly amused):
Read this. (He rips message from teletype, hands it to Fallon.)

116. INSERT   TELETYPE MESSAGE   IN FALLON'S HANDS
      FROM: LEWIS   SPRINGFIELD, ILL.
      TO: EVANS   LOS ANGELES, CALIF.
      POLICE REPORT CODY JARRETT CONFESSION CHECKS
      STOP WILL BE SENTENCED ON TWENTY-EIGHTH STOP

117. BACK TO SCENE:
Fallon, wide-eyed, explodes angrily. Evans watches him, grinning.

FALLON:
Who checks confessions in Springfield? Every rookie in the country knows Scratch Morton went underground after that hotel job! You're not going to let Jarrett get away with a two-bit prison stretch?

EVANS (blandly):
Maybe.

FALLON:
Maybe! A hoodlum turns himself in on a phony rap and beats the gas chamber. I bet right now he's thumbing his nose at Uncle Sam and loving it. Jarrett outsmarted you!

EVANS (softly):
That's just what we want him to think. (Fallon gapes.) We're working *with* the Springfield police. We *arranged* for the confession to check. So what happens? Jarrett does a stretch in the penitentiary . . .

117A. CLOSE SHOT   FALLON
as he begins to get the idea.

EVANS'S VOICE (off-screen; continuing):
And in case he feels lonely—wants to talk to some-

one—we're going to let one of our own boys do a
stretch right in the same cell . . .

FALLON (groaning):
Oh, no! . . . Not again!

117B. TWO-SHOT   EVANS AND FALLON

EVANS (grinning):
You'll enjoy the food in this prison. Wonderful chef.
Arrested him myself.

FALLON (desperately):
Look, Phil—help!

EVANS (sympathetically):
I wouldn't ask you to do another undercover job if
we weren't up against it. But we've got to get Jarrett
and his gang—and to do that we've got to find out
where they unloaded three hundred thousand dollars of federal currency without having a single bill
show up in the usual places. That means you have
to learn the identity of some very special fence.

FALLON:
Any idea how he operates?

EVANS:
I think the answer's Europe. Beautiful setup. Buy
stolen money here at thirty-forty cents on the dollar,
smuggle it out, and peddle it on the European black
market for—who knows how much. And no ques-
tions asked.

FALLON:
Sweet racket. In step with the times.

EVANS:
That's your assignment, Hank. Stick with Cody Jarrett until you find out who the fence is.

Trent enters, carrying a large parcel. He grins at Fallon.

TRENT:

> Your new buddies. Prison records from Illinois.

FALLON:

> Busy little place, isn't it?

TRENT:

> Twenty-seven hundred of the roughest and tough-est.

FALLON:

> And I was all set for a quiet fishing trip up in the mountains.

EVANS:

> You're going fishing. (Unwrapping records.) Through these.

> > DISSOLVE TO:

118.   INT. EVANS'S OFFICE   CLOSE SHOT   NIGHT
shooting over Fallon's shoulder. He sits at Evans's desk, methodically scrutinizing the records of the inmates which are piled in stacks on desk. Each record contains a photo and a case history. Fallon discovers a record that holds his attention.

EVANS'S VOICE:

> Find another old client?

119.   EVANS AND FALLON
Both men are in shirt-sleeves. They have been at it for hours. Evans is preparing some coffee. Fallon hands him a record.

FALLON:

> Red Draper. Questioned him in Forty-six about a warehouse job.

EVANS:

> That makes two for transfer. (Places records to one side.) Better run through the arrest once more.

FALLON (examining records):
I'll be picked up in a joint known as Tom's Hideaway . . .

EVANS:
Bill's Hideaway.

FALLON:
. . . Bill's Hideaway—on what looks like a regular vag roundup. One of the boys spots me as a lamster. I make a break for it. When I pick myself up off the floor I'm meek as a baby. (Puts stack aside.) Nothing more here. (Picks up another pile.) How do I get information out to you?

EVANS:
Visiting days.

FALLON:
Mother again?

EVANS:
Wife this time.

FALLON:
Wife? Fine. Only one thing, Phil . . . this time get someone with a memory. I had awful trouble with "Mother" in San Quentin.

EVANS:
We'll get a girl in the bureau who's a memory expert.

FALLON:
I'm partial to blondes.

EVANS:
Who isn't? Soon as I pick her I'll send you a picture.

Fallon comes across another picture that he recognizes.

FALLON:
Oh—oh! We move this guy.

EVANS:
Who is he?

120. INSERT   CLOSE SHOT   PRISON RECORD OF BO CREEL
In upper left-hand corner is a picture of Bo Creel—thin-lipped, lean-faced. Hold on this insert longer than usual, since we are to meet Bo Creel again.

FALLON'S VOICE:
Bo Creel. Arrested him two years ago.

121. BACK TO SCENE

EVANS (examining Bo's record):
Wait a minute. We don't have to worry about him. Finishes his stretch Saturday. He'll be out before you're sentenced.

FALLON:
Good. Bo Creel would know me in the dark.

Evans puts Bo Creel's record back on the general pile in front of Fallon, who leans back and stretches wearily. Evans pours coffee.[13]

EVANS:
You'd better know what you're walking into Hank. This job won't be like any of your others. You see, there's insanity in the Jarretts, and some of it rubbed off on Cody. His father died in an institution.

FALLON:
I've had a few strange cellmates, in my time, but this looks like the jackpot.

EVANS:
When he was a kid, he used to fake headaches to get his mother's attention away from the rest of the family. It worked. But as he grew up, the fancied headaches became real, until now they tear him apart. Any minute he's likely to crack open at the

seams—and there goes our case. So you'll be working against time.

FALLON:
Suits me. Quicker the better.

EVANS:
Except that Jarrett's not the kind of guy you can get close to in a hurry. The only person he's ever trusted or cared about is his mother. No one else has ever made a dent, not even his wife. His mother's the prop that's always held him up. He's got a fierce, psychopathic devotion for her. All his life, whenever he's been in a spot he's only had to put out his hand . . . and there was Ma Jarrett. Without her, maybe Cody—(Snaps his fingers.) Just like his old man.

FALLON:
You mean I'm supposed to take Mama's place?

EVANS:
You can never tell. He may need someone.

FALLON:
I'll practice up on my lullabies.

EVANS:
Good. Now let's run through your background again.

FALLON (tapping pencil):
Born Detroit, March twenty-third, 1919. State reform school, 1934, vandalism. Arrested suspicion grand larceny, Portland, 1939 . . .

Through this, camera moves in to close of pencil tapping.

DISSOLVE THROUGH TO:

122. INT. SUPERIOR COURT   CLOSE ON GAVEL
in judge's hand as it raps for order. Pull back to reveal

clerk who has risen from his desk. This is the day when previously convicted prisoners are sentenced.

CLERK:
 The State of Illinois versus Arthur Cody Jarrett.

123. CLOSE ON CODY
 Relaxed, confident, Cody rises and steps in front of the judge's bench.

JUDGE:
 Arthur Cody Jarrett . . . on your own admission you have been convicted of the robbery of the Palace Hotel on the night of October twelfth, and it is now my duty to pronounce sentence. For the crime of grand larceny you are hereby sentenced to serve not less than one and not more than three years in the state penitentiary.

A bailiff starts to lead him away.

CLERK:
 The State of Illinois versus Victor Pardo.

Hank Fallon rises. He is Vic Pardo and will be so designated for the remainder of the script.

VIC (passing Cody):
 How is he? Tough?

Cody brushes by him without answering.[14]

FADE OUT

FADE IN
124. EXT. PENITENTIARY (STOCK SHOT)   DAY
                                  DISSOLVE THROUGH TO:

125. EXT. PRISON COURTYARD   DAY
 crowded with prisoners. It is the midday "break."
                                  DISSOLVE THROUGH TO:

126. EXT. PRISON COURTYARD   MED. GROUP OF PRISONERS
 around Roy Parker, a thin-lipped con, about forty.

PARKER:

> With Big Ed givin' the orders now there'll be all kinds
> of fireworks. He's got plans will make the old Jarrett
> mob look like schoolkids. Ed's got polish.

127.   MED. GROUP   CODY, READER, RYLEY, VIC
about fifteen feet from above group. Tommy Ryley, a
trusty, is playing cards with Cody, with cigarettes as
stakes. Vic leans against the wall, watching them. The
Reader, an old lifer who has mastered lipreading, wears
a hearing aid.

CODY:

> Can you read him?

READER:

> Yeah. Parker moves his lips pretty good. It's about
> Big Ed.

CODY:

> What about him?

READER:

> He's number-one boy now, Parker says.

CODY:

> Big Ed always did have big ideas.

READER:

> In more ways than one, Parker says.

Cody's hand pauses in the act of pocketing cigarettes
which he has won.

128.   PARKER'S GROUP   (CODY'S ANGLE)
Parker says something. His audience laughs obscenely.

129.   CODY'S ANGLE

CODY:

> What was that crack?

READER (lying):
　　I—I couldn't see him, Cody.

CODY:
　　Was it about my wife?

READER:
　　Honest, Cody . . . he had his mouth covered.

CODY (rising):
　　Maybe a kick in the skull will teach him some man-
　　ners.

VIC:
　　They got rules in this chicken coop, Cody. Start any-
　　thing and ya wind up in the hole.

CODY:
　　Who asked you for advice? (Vic shrugs.) Listen,
　　Pardo, I been watchin' ya. So far ya ain't done nothin'
　　I can put my finger on, but maybe that's what both-
　　ers me. I don't know ya, and what I don't know I
　　don't trust. To me ya're just a number and a face,
　　and for now keep it that way. When I need your
　　help I'll ask for it.

VIC (conciliatory):
　　Have it your way, Cody.

Suddenly a commanding voice is heard coming through
the courtyard loudspeaker.

VOICE:
　　Attention! Attention!

130.　LOUDSPEAKER HORN
　　set on the courtyard wall. From it emerges:

VOICE:
　　The following new men report to the dispensary for
　　shots. Abbott, Jules; Bacon, James; Butler, Fred . . .

　　　　　　　　　　　　　　　　　　DISSOLVE TO:

131.   INT. PRISON HOSPITAL WARD   CLOSE SHOT   CONVICT
wincing as a needle is jabbed into his arm. Over shot:

RYLEY'S VOICE:
   Hall, Robert!

                                              DRAW BACK TO:

132.   FULL SHOT   (SHOOTING PAST DOCTOR)
Lined up alphabetically, jackets over their left arms, the
convicts single-file past prison doctor who administers
the shots. To the doctor's left, backs to camera, are two
convict trusties. The first is Tommy Ryley, who calls off
the names and checks them off, upon which the designated convict takes two more paces which bring him
before the second trusty, who stands by a small table
and dabs alcohol on the arms where the needle will be
inserted by the doctor. The names are called by Ryley
through this scene: "Holden, John; Hughes, Russell;
Hide, Frank; Jackson, William; Jacoby, George;" etc. Two
guards supervise the formation, maintaining silence and
hustling the laggards.

A GUARD:
   Keep it moving! No talking!

133.   MED. SHOT   CODY   IN LINE
He shuffles forward obediently. Move down line to pick
up Vic Pardo, shuffling forward like the others. Behind
him in line is Roy Parker. Vic looks ahead over the
shoulder of the man in front of him, sees something that
makes him catch his breath.

TRUSTY'S VOICE:
   Hughes, Russell!

134.   CLOSE SHOT   RUSSELL HUGHES
As his name is called and checked off by Ryley, Hughes
steps up into camera proffering his right arm for the dab
of alcohol. As the second trusty's hand comes into shot

to perform the task, Hughes stares, surprised. (NOTE: Talking is forbidden; these scenes played in whispers.)

HUGHES:
>If it ain't Bo Creel . . .

Pan to close on second trusty. He is *Bo Creel*.

HUGHES'S VOICE (continuing):
>. . . The boys in L.A. had a comin' out party planned for ya a month ago.

BO CREEL (dabbing Hughes's arm):
>Yeah. I was packin' and—bang!—flat on my back with pneumonia. Doc's checkin' me out today.

HUGHES'S VOICE:
>Well, see ya in eight years.

135.   MED. CLOSE   VIC PARDO AND ROY PARKER
Vic has involuntarily stopped his slow forward motion. Parker is crowding him.

PARKER:
>Get the lead out.

Vic inhales deeply, shuffles forward in line.

136.   FULL SHOT   (SHOOTING PAST CREEL ALONG CONVICT LINE)
Cody is now second in line. A little further back is Vic Pardo, helplessly shuffling toward the moment when he may be unmasked.

RYLEY:
>Jarrett, Arthur Cody.

Cody takes two steps up to Bo Creel.

137.   CODY AND BO CREEL

BO CREEL:
>I'm leavin' tomorrow, Cody. Anything I can do for ya on the Coast?

CODY:
   When ya see Big Ed, tell him I was askin' for him.

Bo nods. Cody moves toward doctor.

RYLEY'S VOICE:
   Matthews, Daniel!

138.   MED. CLOSE   VIC PARDO AND ROY PARKER
   with Bo Creel in shot, only separated from Vic now by
   three cons in the line. Vic, desperate, looks away as
   though trying to delay the moment of inevitable recognition. Again he lags. Roy Parker pushes him roughly.

PARKER:
   Scared, sonny?

It is Vic's cue. Suddenly he whirls on Parker, punching
him savagely on the mouth, then closing with him and
dragging him to the ground, where they pound each
other.

139.   THREE FLASHES
   Cody, in the act of putting on his jacket, pauses to watch
   the brawl; Bo Creel, standing on tiptoe, craning to see;
   guard, running forward.

140.   MED.   VIC AND PARKER
   scrapping on the floor. Vic has acquired a bleeding nose.
   The guard rushes into shot, tugs at Vic.

PARKER:
   I didn't do nothin'! He's nuts!

GUARD (jerks Vic to his feet):
   A little solitary'll cool you off, slugger.

DISSOLVE TO:[15]

141.   INT. CELLBLOCK   MED. SHOT   GUARD
   distributing mail, which has been opened for censor-
   ship. He pauses at a four-bunk second-tier cell occupied

by Cody, Reader, and Tommy Ryley. Cody lies on a bunk, disinterested. Reader and Ryley eagerly take their letters as they are passed through bars.

GUARD:
> Ryley—Curtin . . . (A big envelope.) Pardo.

RYLEY (grand manner):
> I'm awfully sorry, my good man, but Mr. Pardo's still on vacation.

GUARD:
> His month's up today.

142.   INT. CELL   MED. FULL SHOT

CODY:
> It is, huh? That's cozy.

As guard goes out of shot, the Reader puts Vic's envelope beside him on bunk, reads his own letter.

RYLEY:
> Lookit what they left of this one. Musta been a lulu before the warden got it. (He holds up a drastically scissor-censored letter.)

CODY:
> Say, Reader, any chance ya get, read Pardo, will ya?

READER:
> Maybe visitin' day. That's when they unbend.

RYLEY:
> What ya got against him, Cody? Pardo's okay. Didn't I check his record up in the dispensary?

CODY:
> That's just a record. What else do we know about him? Maybe his letter will tell us somethin'. Let's have it, Reader.

READER (doubtfully):
> Ya think ya should? It's U.S. mail.

CODY:
I'm a U.S. citizen, ain't I?

RYLEY:
Not lately.

With some misgivings the Reader passes Cody the envelope. Cody extracts a photograph.

143.   INSERT   PHOTOGRAPH IN CODY'S HANDS
It is a portrait of Margaret Baxter, inscribed "Your loving wife, Betty."

144.   MED. SHOT
Cody passes the picture and envelope to the Reader.

READER:
Wife, huh? The kid don't talk much.

RYLEY:
When ya married ya don't have a chance to. (Looks at picture.) Nice!

CODY:
Put her up on the bureau where we can all get a look at her.

READER (troubled):
He'll know we been in his mail.

CODY:
So he'll know.

RYLEY (sentimentally):
Be a nice surprise after solitary. (He puts the portrait on the bureau.)

145.   INT. CELLBLOCK   (SHOOTING TOWARD CELL FLOOR)
camera rises with Vic Pardo and a guard as they mount circular stairway to second tier, and then moves with them along to the cell, where guard opens door.

146.   INT. CELL
as Vic enters and the guard goes out of shot.

RYLEY:
Hi, kid.

READER:
Let me shake the hand that slugged Roy Parker.

CODY:
Why'd ya do it, Pardo? They got rules in this chicken
coop, remember?

VIC:
Maybe I didn't wanta get my shots.

Vic senses something strange in the way they grin at
him and at each other, but can't put his finger on it. As
he looks from one to the other, his glance passes photo,
but it means nothing.

CODY:
Maybe his eyes ain't so good, after solitary.

VIC:
What's the gag?

He is now acutely aware of the others' exchange of looks.
He senses the danger of the unknown. Then his eyes
see something in the corner of the bunk.

147.   CLOSE ON ENVELOPE
It is addressed "Mr. Vic Pardo, State Penitentiary, Ill."
(In top left corner stamped in block letters are the words
Photo—Do Not Bend.)

148.   MED. SHOT
Vic gives no indication that he has caught on from the
envelope. But he suddenly strides to the bureau, with
an exclamation of surprise, grabs photo.

VIC:

> Hey! What's she done to herself? The best-looking blonde you ever saw—and the second my back's turned she goes brunette! Why, it don't even look like her anymore!

The others are amused at Vic's consternation, but accept it.

READER:

> Maybe she's hot.

RYLEY:

> Yeah. Whenever I changed my hair so did my missus.

VIC:

> She better be a blonde again when I get outa here. (He puts photo back on bureau, clambers up to his berth.)

149.   CLOSE-UP   VIC
stretching out, breathing an inaudible sigh of relief.

CODY'S VOICE:

> Say, Pardo . . .

150.   CODY AND THE READER   (SHOOTING UP TOWARD VIC'S BUNK)
A humorless grin on Cody's lips.

CODY:

> . . . Too bad your sluggin' Parker didn't work.

Vic, on thin ice again, rolls over into shot, to look down at others. He grunts inquiringly.

151.   GROUP
Vic sees the exchange of grins again, tenses.

RYLEY (up to Vic):

> The doc says you gotta take your shots anyway.

Cody chuckles. He enjoys the joke enormously.

152.   CLOSE-UP   VIC
He chuckles, too, but more wryly than they.

153.   FULL SHOT
A rapping is heard, caused by someone signaling from the next cell. This is a cue for the Reader, who goes to front corner of cell and holds a small mirror outside bars so that he may see the lips of a convict in adjoining cell.

154.   CLOSE   READER AND CONVICT

READER:
   Yeah, Benny?

The convict talks soundlessly, moves his lips in exaggerated fashion to facilitate Reader's job.

155.   CLOSE-UP MIRROR   (IN READER'S HAND)
In the mirror the convict's lips are seen moving.

156.   FULL SHOT
The message delivered, Reader waves thanks, turns back.

READER:
   Parker's been shootin' off his mouth again. Told Benny your boys pulled a caper.

CODY:
   What'd they get?

READER:
   Fifty-seven grand.

CODY:
   Not bad.

RYLEY:
   You in for any of it, Cody?

CODY:
> Full share.

VIC (leaning over):
> No kiddin'?

RYLEY:
> Why not? What's bein' in here got to do with it? They're still his boys, ain't they? What they get, Cody gets.

CODY:
> Ma sees to that.

DISSOLVE TO:

157.   INT. HOUSE   HIGH ANGLE   GROUP SHOT   NIGHT
Around a table are grouped Big Ed, Cotton, Happy, Het, and Ma Jarrett, upon whom their attention is centered. On table before her are five neat stacks of bills, all the same size. Verna watches closely from couch.

MA JARRETT:
> . . . The Trader does business right. It didn't make any difference I was a woman. The Trader's a gentleman. Gave me the same price as if he was doin' business with Cody himself. (Through this she has distributed four of the stacks, one to each man, leaving one stack remaining on the table. The men hold their money and their eyes stare as one at the remaining stack. Ma sees this; her mouth tightens.) Anything wrong?

COTTON:
> Who's that for?

MA JARRETT:
> Cody! Who'd you think?

HET:
> Pretty healthy cut. While we were riskin' our necks to heist this dough, Cody was sittin' it out.

MA JARRETT (contemptuously):
Greedy, ain't you? So that's all you think he was doin'!
Why, when Cody took that rap he cleared all of you
for the tunnel job. He didn't ask no one else to do
it, did he? That's how Cody is. He wanted to keep
the mob goin'. And you say he's just sittin' it out.

HET (uncomfortably):
I was only askin'.[16]

MA JARRETT (hard):
All of you—get one thing straight. Anything we get,
Cody's in for his full share. And that's how it is.
Anybody thinks different, just say so now. Or would
you rather wait till Cody gets out? Well, any argu-
ment?

158.   PANNING SHOT   GROUP OF MEN
They are silent as camera picks up each of them in turn.

MA'S VOICE:
Het? . . . Cotton? . . . Happy? . . . Ed? . . .

159.   GROUP   (VERNA IN BACKGROUND)
Ma looks at Big Ed with ill-concealed contempt.

MA:
How come, Ed? You're the one I expected to give
trouble.

BIG ED (with a shrug):
Fair's fair. We ain't gonna forget Cody after all he
did for us.

MA:
Cody'll be real grateful to you.

Verna, looking sullen, rises, snaps an angry glance at
Big Ed and starts out.

111

MA:
> Where do you think you're goin'?

VERNA:
> To see if the sky's still there. I'm worried about it.

Ma glares after her as she exits, the men watching her hips with no little interest.

MA (picks up Cody's stack):
> All right, boys, beat it. It's gettin' late. Het, tell Verna I want her back in here.

Het nods as the men start out.

160.   EXT. PORCH   NEAR STEPS   NIGHT
As men come out Verna is seen leaning sulkily against porch railing, smoking a cigarette. Big Ed lingers so that he is behind the others.

HET:
> Ma wants ya inside. (Goes out of shot.)

VERNA:
> She's afraid maybe I'll get some fresh air in my lungs.

The others have exited shot. Now Big Ed comes up to Verna. They talk in low voices.

BIG ED:
> What's eatin' ya, sugar?

VERNA:
> You and your big ideas! That's all they are—ideas! "You and me belong, together, sugar. Just leave it to Big Ed." Well, I'm sick of waitin' for ya to make your move! You're as scared of Cody as any of them. He's still Mr. Big—in prison or out.

BIG ED:
> What makes ya think so?

VERNA:
"Fair's fair," is it? That was quite a beef you put up about Cody bein' in on the cut.

BIG ED:
A man thinks his pals are takin' care of him—he gets careless.

VERNA:
What's that mean?

BIG ED (slowly):
Alive, Cody gets out in maybe two years. Dead, he gets out sooner.

VERNA:
Dead . . .

BIG ED:
He's a sittin' duck up there in the pen. Right now he's rubbin' shoulders with a guy who does anything I say.

VERNA (after a pause; low):
When, Ed?

BIG ED:
When I tell him.

Grips her arm in a gesture of reassurance and ardor.[17] She looks up at him. He starts off. Pan over to window and dolly in swiftly to show Ma Jarrett peering out at them through a chink in the blinds.

DISSOLVE TO:

161.   INT. PENITENTIARY MACHINE SHOP   DAY
Lathes, stamps, presses, drills, boring machines, etc. The whirr of machinery, the din of metal against metal. From a raised platform a guard supervises. Another guard makes the rounds on the floor.

113

162. FULL SHOT   CODY
His job is to collect the small trash bins containing metal shavings, etc., from lathes and benches, load them onto a low wagon, and eventually empty them into a larger trash bin. He now moves from one worker to another, loading the wagon with small bins.

163. MED. SHOT   VIC PARDO
repairing a transformer at a workbench. A foreman enters shot carrying a portable radio.

FOREMAN:
You know so much about radios, maybe you can fix the warden's.

VIC:
I'll fix it so it blows up in his face.

Foreman grins, goes. Vic removes back of radio. He sees something off-screen, turns. Pan to:

164. MED. SHOT   ROY PARKER
He comes up to a big metal trash bin, the main receptacle, about six feet from Vic's bench. Parker, thinking himself unobserved, moves the bin a foot to one side, looks up above him, then, with a grim look of satisfaction, goes out of shot.

165. MED. SHOT   VIC PARDO
Puzzled by Parker's action, he glances upward.

166. WHAT VIC SEES
A monorail used for transporting heavy weights and equipment is directly above the bin.

167. MED. SHOT   VIC
Frowning, he returns to work on radio.

114

168.   MED. SHOT   PARKER
coming to the other end of the monorail, from which a
claw pulley hangs, controlled by a winch which Parker
operates. He hooks the claws to a heavy transformer
weighing several hundred pounds, looks off.

169.   CODY   (PARKER'S ANGLE)
He lifts another small trash bin onto the wagon. This
completes the load, and now Cody begins to drag the
wagon to the big trash bin near Vic.

170.   MED. SHOT   PARKER
as he operates the winch. The transformer is slowly lifted
as high as it will go, then responding to Parker's control
begins to creep along monorail in direction taken by Cody.

171.   DOLLY SHOT   AHEAD OF CODY   (LOW ANGLE)
To include monorail, as he pulls wagon, unaware that
the transformer is keeping pace with him above and behind.

172.   CLOSE SHOT   PARKER
like a man who has drawn a bead on a sitting duck.

173.   HIGH ANGLE   MOVING SHOT   CODY
Shooting down past traveling transformer. Cody reaches
big trash bin, stops, empties first small bin into it.

174.   MED.   VIC
He finishes examining radio. In need of a tool he climbs
on a box and reaches into machinists'-type pigeonholes.
His attention is arrested by something off-screen. He
looks down at Cody's position off-screen, then up at the
transformer's position off-screen.

175.   CLOSE   PARKER
He throws the control to release the hooks.

176.   CLOSE-UP   HOOKS HOLDING TRANSFORMER
as they disengage.

177.   CLOSE   CODY
emptying another small bin. Suddenly Vic hurtles into shot, upending Cody. As they both tumble to ground out of shot, the transformer crashes down.

178.   FLASH SHOT
Transformer crashing to floor.

179.   MED.   CODY AND VIC
Cody has hit his forehead in the fall. Dazed, he pushes Vic, swings his arm as if to strike him. Then he realizes what happened, and his mouth tightens as he stares at bin.

180.   CLOSE SHOT   BIN
crushed flat beneath the transformer.

181.   CLOSE   PARKER
sudden fear crossing his face.

182.   FULL SHOT
as guard pushes through convicts who have rushed up.

GUARD:
Back to your places! Nobody's hurt. (Calls.) Parker!

Parker enters shot, frightened.

PARKER (trembling):
Nobody's   fault—it   was   an   accident—lever slipped . . .

GUARD:
You can tell it to the warden later. (To group.) Back to your places! (They drift away.) You all right, Jarrett?

116

CODY:
Sure. It was gettin' dull around here.

GUARD:
Back to work. You, too, Pardo. (Leaves.)

183.   VIC AND CODY

VIC:
I saw that just in time.

CODY:
What do you want—a medal?

VIC (shrugging):
You woulda looked like that bin.

CODY (looking at him):
You almost walked into it yourself. Why should you care if a guy called Cody Jarrett gets his? Unless ya want something?

VIC:
Okay, keep your medal.

CODY:
And you keep to yourself. Get it?

Their eyes hold for a moment, then Vic half-smiles, shrugs and moves away, back to his workbench.

183A.   CLOSE ON CODY
He turns, looks speculatively off-screen, then walks slowly toward Parker, camera trucking. It is difficult to tell what Cody is thinking.

183B.   MED.   PARKER
A sick smile crosses his face. Cody enters shot and Parker's hands tremble on the lever he is operating. He speaks quickly, nervously.

PARKER:
I'm—sorry, Cody. Glad you weren't hurt.

CODY (his smile friendly yet enigmatic):
Forget it, Parker. Accidents'll happen.

Parker blinks.

184.   GUARD ON RAISED PLATFORM   NEAR DOOR
He speaks into a microphone, reading from a list.

GUARD:
The following men have visitors . . . Reynolds, Allen, Jarrett . . .

185.   CODY (PANNING)
His brows knit. A visitor? Slowly, he starts for door. The two other men are seen approaching door.

DISSOLVE TO:

186.   INT. VISITING ROOM   SHOOTING UP AT SIGN
nailed above door, reading Visitors Are Forbidden To Touch Wire Screen. Pan down to show one of the men from machine shop as he comes through door and is motioned to a seat by a guard. Truck with convict as he moves to designated seat, revealing normal visiting room setup. Chairs on either side of wire screen. A few convicts already with their visitors. As convict sits camera continues past him and holds on Ma Jarrett, waiting on other side of screen. Dolly in to show the degree of anxiety under which she labors. Her hands wash each other compulsively, her lips are dry, there is fear in her eyes. Suddenly her hands are still. She tries desperately to compose herself.

187.   MED. CLOSE PANNING ON CODY
as he crosses visiting room toward chair pointed out to him by guard. He sees that Ma is his visitor. The pause in his stride is barely perceptible.

188.   CODY AND MA
As Cody comes in Ma manages a stiff smile.

CODY:
> Hello, Ma.

MA (sees his forehead):
> Cody— you been hurt.

CODY:
> It's nothin'. An accident.

MA:
> You sure?

CODY:
> What kinda question is that? What're ya so nervous about? (Looks at her.) Anything wrong?

MA (under strain):
> Plenty.

CODY:
> For instance?

MA (with difficulty):
> I knew you'd hear anyhow, Cody. That's why I came. I'm the one to tell you. It's Big Ed and Verna. They ran out.

189.   CLOSE ON CODY
His face goes stony.

MA'S VOICE:
> It's my fault, Cody. I let you down. I said I'd take care of things. But I let you down.

190.   CODY AND MA

MA:
> I saw it comin' only I didn't think he had the guts.

CODY (tightly):
Forget it, Ma. It was in the cards for Big Ed to make his try.

MA (incredulously):
Don't you care?

CODY (hard):
Sure, I care! What's mine's mine! But I ain't gonna get sick about it. I'll catch up to 'em when I get out.

MA (relieved):
That's just what I told myself. And I'll help you— like always. You'll be out soon—back on top of the world.

CODY:
With you around, Ma, nothin' can stop me.

MA:
That's right, Cody. Except you've gotta be careful.

CODY:
Careful?

MA:
About Big Ed.

CODY (chuckles):
If I know Big Ed he's doin' enough worryin' now for both of us.

MA:
Maybe not.

CODY:
Ya think he don't expect I'll come after him?

MA:
That's what I'm gettin' at, Cody. He knows when you get out his life won't be worth a plugged nickel. When a tinhorn thinks he's big enough to take your place, he's gotta feel pretty safe. But now, all of a

sudden, he makes his move, just like he's sure you're *never* gettin' out of here—except in a box.

CODY:

Yeah . . . I see what ya mean. (Fingers bump on head.)

MA:

You said it was an accident.

CODY:

For a minute I thought it was.

MA:

How'd it happen?

CODY:

A pal of Big Ed's dropped somethin'.

MA (alarmed):

You see, Cody—I was right! He was figurin' you'd be dead.

CODY:

Relax, Ma. I'm here, ain't I?

MA:

If he tried once—he'll try again.

CODY:

I'll still *walk* out of this joint. Then I'll take care of Big Ed.

MA:

And let him live that long? (Deadly.) I'll take care of him, Cody.

CODY:

No, Ma! Ya won't have a chance!

MA:

Any time I can't handle his kind, I'll know I'm gettin' old. Nobody does what he did to you and gets away with it.

CODY:
> I'm tellin' ya—don't . . .

MA (rising):
> I'm goin' after him, Cody . . . to keep him from havin'
> you knocked off in here.

CODY:
> Don't do it, Ma, ya hear me! Listen . . .

MA:
> Goodbye, Cody.

CODY (a choking cry):
> Ma!

But Ma has gone. Cody claws the screen, face con-
torted. A guard comes up, pulls him away from screen.

GUARD:
> Against the rules to touch the screen. Come on. Back
> to work.

Jaws clenched, Cody suffers himself to be led away.

> DISSOLVE TO:

191.   INT. MACHINE SHOP
Cody enters, face dark, brooding.

192.   PARKER
working the controls, sees Cody off-screen. He stiffens;
his hands tremble involuntarily on the levers.

193.   PAN SHOT   CODY
over to Parker. Cody affects a very friendly manner.

CODY (smiling):
> What's botherin' ya, Parker? I'm not gonna do any-
> thing now. I'm gonna let ya sweat it out. Stay awake
> nights. Until I'm ready to pay ya back. (He moves
> away, grabbing handle of wagon.)

194.   DOLLY SHOT—CODY
thinking. Ma's in danger. Well, Ma can take care of herself. Yeah, but what if she can't? Ma's voice comes over,
hollow, grotesque, with a rhythmic beat: "I'll take care
of him, Cody—I'll take care of him, Cody." He moistens
his lips, frightened, shakes his head as though to silence her voice, but it persists. He stops near Vic's
worktable. Everything begins to blur. The machinery assumes fantastic shapes, weaving, looming up over him,
threatening, closing in. And then the pain begins. The
blinding pain that shuts out the world.

195.   CLOSE-UP   CODY
breathing heavily, fighting back the pain.

196.   MED. CLOSE ON VIC
who glances over at Cody, puzzled by what he sees. Cody
enters shot, staggering against Vic's workbench. It is a
losing fight. His head huddles close to the bench; his
hands, rigid, clutch a vise.

197.   EXTREME CLOSE-UP   CODY
His brow is beaded. Tip down a little to show his face
in profile, creases at the corners of his eyes as he tightens his muscles against the surging pain. Draw back as
Vic bends down quickly into shot.

CODY:
Cover for me! . . . Cover for me! . . .

Cody sinks to his knees. Vic pulls him over to workbench, then looks quickly around.

198.   MED. SHOT   GUARD   (VIC'S ANGLE)
on one of his periodic rounds, coming toward camera.

199.   VIC AND CODY
He hisses warning to Cody.

123

VIC:
>   Watch it!

Vic quickly upsets a toolbox on floor between them. He starts restoring tools to the box. He slips a wrench into Cody's hand, guides it to the box. Guard's legs enter shot. Both convicts—Cody with a supreme effort—are picking up the spilled tools.

VIC (looking up):
>   Fingers are kinda thick today.

200.   CLOSE ON GUARD
He accepts the explanation, continues on his round.

201.   VIC AND CODY   (LOW ANGLE)
Cody, the headache still hammering at him, crouches on the floor like an animal in pain.

CODY:
>   No doctor . . . no doctor . . .

VIC:
>   It's all right. He's gone. (Leaning over Cody.) Where's the pain?

Cody points. Vic's fingers go to the source of the pain. He rubs—harder, harder—always making certain they are unobserved. As he does so:

VIC:
>   Come on, Cody, don't let it beat ya! You're top man, aren't ya? Why, I been readin' about ya since I was a kid, always hopin' I could join up with ya. Ya don't want those two-bit mugs to see Cody Jarrett down on his knees, do ya?

During this, under the ministration of the rubbing and Vic's words, the headache has started to go as swiftly as it came. Cody's breathing becomes more regular, though still heavy. He slowly regains self-control. As Vic finishes talking, Cody, resenting any man's interference, pushes him roughly away. But even as he does so a transference is effected within his mind and he stares at Vic, wide-eyed. He shakes his head as if to toss off the final remnants of the headache, allows Vic to help him to his feet. Their eyes hold for a moment. Then slowly Cody extends his hand. Vic's hand comes out to meet it. The handclasp is a declaration of friendship. Vic grins at him, as we

DISSOLVE TO:

202. SKY   NIGHT
Moon and stars. Draw back to reveal that camera has been shooting through barred prison window. Cody is lying awake on his cot.

203. CODY
face grim, as thoughts about Ma race through his mind. Finally, he swings his feet out, rises, goes to window (camera panning), stares out.

204. WIDER ANGLE
as Vic leans out from his top bunk. They talk in whispers.

VIC:
    You all right, Cody?

CODY (without turning):
    Can't sleep, that's all.

VIC:
    Headache gone?

CODY:
    Yeah.

A pause. Vic senses Cody's vulnerability.

VIC:
    Well, why can't ya sleep?

CODY (turns):
 It's Ma. She's walkin' into trouble.

VIC:
 Anything I can do?

Cody shakes his head. Then, suddenly deciding to trust
Vic, he moves in to him.

CODY:
 Yeah, maybe there is. Look, kid. For a while I figured on sittin' out this penny-ante stretch . . .

205. CLOSE ON CODY

CODY (continuing):
 . . . This was gonna be a vacation. Take the heat off
 me for another job. But sometimes ya make plans
 and they don't work out. What's gotta be done's gotta
 be done—fast. Understand?

206. CODY AND VIC

VIC (shakes head):
 Uh-uh.

CODY:
 I got business on the outside.

VIC (controls excitement):
 A crash-out?

CODY (nodding):
 Wanta come along?

VIC:
 Maybe I do. Ya told anybody else?

CODY:
 No, but I figured we cut in Tommy Ryley.

VIC:
 Ya cut in one and before ya know it it's ten. What do
 ya want Ryley for?

CODY:
> He's got a gun stashed.

VIC:
> Don't need a gun.

CODY:
> They ain't gonna open the doors for us.

Vic looks at Ryley and Reader, apparently to make sure they are sleeping; actually he has to formulate a crude plan in a matter of seconds. Turns back to Cody.

VIC:
> You ain't the only guy in this parlor wants out. What do ya think *I* been dreamin' of nights? I got a way of gettin' a mile from here before anybody knows what hit 'em.

CODY:
> Without artillery? Can't be done.

VIC:
> No? I'm pretty handy around electricity, remember? Well, I figured a way to fix the generators. Know what that means?

CODY (slowly; admiringly):
> Yeah, I got a faint idea.

VIC:
> The generators control everything. Searchlights. Gun turrets. Main gate. Who needs artillery? But we gotta do it alone.

CODY (accepting this):
> We'll need a car.

VIC:
> My wife's comin' tomorrow. We'll set it all up.

CODY:
> All right, kid. It's a deal. (They shake hands.) If it works, I'll pay ya back.

VIC:
> Maybe ya'll give me that medal?

CODY (with a grin):
> Solid gold.

As Cody gets back into his bunk Vic can hardly conceal his excitement. He's got Cody just where he wants him.[18]

DISSOLVE TO:

207.   INT. VISITING ROOM   READER AND LAWYER   DAY
The lawyer is a scrawny, sharp-faced man.

LAWYER:
> Good news for you, Herbert.

READER:
> You've had good news for the last twelve years.

LAWYER:
> I'm working on a plan to get your case reviewed.

During this the Reader's eyes follow someone off-screen.

208.   MOVING SHOT   VIC   (READER'S ANGLE)
as he goes to vacant chair. Through the wire screen can be seen Margaret Baxter, his "wife." She is young, self-possessed, brunette.

209.   VIC AND MARGARET
In background Reader can be seen, his eyes never leaving them.

VIC (normal voice):
> Hello, Margaret.

MARGARET:
> You're looking well, Vic.

VIC (hand to side of mouth; low):
> We're being watched. Say anything you like. Make it sound good. And listen to me carefully.

MARGARET (after split-second pause):
>Divorce! Vic, you can't mean that! Why? What have I done? (She pauses, her eyes searching if her line of talk is okay.)

VIC (who keeps his lips screened throughout):
>That's fine . . . Jarrett's getting out of here and I'm going with him.

MARGARET:
>I know how you feel, Vic. But don't ask me to do anything that will break my heart.

VIC (turns to be sure the Reader sees his lips):
>It might be better for you.

MARGARET:
>But it's my life. Let me decide what to do with it.

VIC (turns back to Margaret):
>Just the two of us. Tell Evans we'll break Thursday night.

MARGARET:
>Do you think I'm the kind to run out just because you got a bad break?

VIC:
>Tell him to plant a getaway car—with an oscillator. Will you remember that? An *oscillator*.

MARGARET:
>I'll remember, darling.

210.   READER AND LAWYER

LAWYER:
>. . . and this time I'm going right to the top to get you out . . . Herbert, are you listening?

READER (still looking off-screen):
>Sure, Jerry, sure.[19]

211.   MARGARET AND VIC

VIC:
Everything clear?

MARGARET:
Perfectly clear.

VIC:
Come back next visiting day.

MARGARET:
You won't be sorry, Vic. When you get out, we'll be happy. I'll make you happy.[20]

VIC (grinning):
Nice going. Where'd you hear all that—soap opera?

MARGARET:
How did you know?

Guard enters shot, taps Vic on shoulder.

GUARD:
Sorry Pardo. There's a mob waiting.

MARGARET (as Vic rises):
Goodbye, darling. Good luck.

VIC:
Goodbye, Betty.

212.   READER AND LAWYER

LAWYER:
. . . But if that fails, you'll just have to serve the rest of your term.

The guard has entered shot, and taps Reader's shoulder.

White Heat

READER (rising):
Jerry, you couldn't get me out of here if I was pardoned.

DISSOLVE TO[21]

213. INT. EVANS'S OFFICE   CLOSE   MAP ON DESK   DAY
Small-scale map of the penitentiary and environs, on which Evans's pencil draws marks to illustrate.

EVANS'S VOICE:
Now, we place the getaway car in these trees, with the oscillator under its rear axle and hooked to the battery. Our cars will be parked back here a mile or so away—one here, the other here . . . We assume Jarrett and Hank come out here somewhere.

214. GROUP—EVANS, DONOVAN, CLARK, ERNIE TRENT
On corner of desk stands a shortwave radio receiver. In a corner of the room, Trent hooks up midget electronics instrument. Donovan and Clark flank Evans at desk.

EVANS:
They pile in the getaway car, and they're off. Ready, Ernie?

TRENT:
Ready. Transmitter wavelength forty-seven one.

EVANS (adjusts receiver):
Forty-seven one. Switch it on. (Trent obeys. From loudspeaker emerges transmission radio signal, a high, singing sound.) Our receivers pick up that signal from the oscillator, enabling us to crossplot their exact position.

215. INSERT   MAP ON DESK
Evans's pencil draws short lines radiating from getaway car to other cars.

EVANS'S VOICE (continuing):
>For example, the impulse received here has a bearing of two hundred twenty-five degrees; the one here reads twelve degrees. We plot them—like so—and where the lines cross, that's where they are.

216.   BACK TO SCENE

EVANS (continuing):
>Doesn't matter how far they travel. As long as our cars are within receiving distance we can tell where they are . . . Cut it, Ernie.

Trent switches off transmitter, ending signal; through following he disconnects instrument and brings it to desk.

CLARK:
>How far is receiving distance?

EVANS:
>We had a dry run yesterday and kept tabs on a moving car twenty miles away.

DONOVAN (points to transmitter):
>That little thing?

TRENT:
>You could make one out of your bedside radio. All you do is disconnect—

EVANS:
>Sometime when you've got a week to spare, Ernie'll tell you all about electronics. (Looks at watch.) We'll meet at the airport in forty minutes. Be in Springfield late this afternoon.

>>DISSOLVE TO:

217.   INT. PRISON MESS HALL   DAY
Four hundred prisoners file in, in a double line. Each table accommodates twenty-four, twelve on either side. At a whistle the prisoners break off, right flank and left flank, and stand before their places.

218.   THE TABLES   SIDE ANGLE
Vic and Cody in foreground face each other across table.

219.   VIC
He nods almost imperceptibly, mouths: "Tonight."

220.   CODY
returns the nod.

221.   THE TABLE   HIGH ANGLE
Another whistle. The men sit, begin to eat. The clatter of dishes and utensils. (NOTE: Talking at mealtime is forbidden so the following exchange is played in a whisper.) Cody looks down toward end of table at a new prisoner (Lefeld), who eats greedily. Cody inclines his head slightly to Ryley beside him.

222.   CODY AND RYLEY

CODY:
Ain't that Nat Lefeld?

RYLEY:
From the coast mob. Came in today.

CODY:
Ask him if he saw my mother.

Ryley nods, half-turns to the man on his right. His lips move, but his voice is inaudible.

223.   MOVING SHOT   ALONG ROW OF MEN AT TABLE
as the question is silently passed along, each man turning his head slightly to the man on his right. Finally, camera holds as the question is put to Lefeld, at end of table. He whispers an answer to the man on his left, who, first giving him a long look, turns to pass the message back. Camera, almost as if it were the message itself, moves back along the row of prisoners until Ryley

receives it. His jaw drops. Cody looks at him penetrat-
ingly.

RYLEY (low):
  She's dead.

224. CLOSE ON CODY
He sits stunned, rigid under the impact. Every muscle
in his body tenses as he tries in vain to reject the tragic
news. Then his taut face seems to crumple. His eyes are
dilated, mouth open, lips drawn back. *Dead! Ma dead!*
Involuntarily his hand crushes the tin drinking cup he
holds. From his throat issues an atavistic scream—prim-
itive, bestial, inhuman. Instantly there is absolute *silence*—not even the rattle of a fork.

225. THE TABLE   HIGH ANGLE   FEATURING CODY
Cody, his reason gone, stumbles to his feet, flings the
drinking cup across the room, mouthing guttural ani-
mallike sounds. Two guards have started forward. Cody
lurches away from the table, heading toward the entrance. A guard looms up before him. Cody throws a
cruel punch against the guard's jaw. The man drops,
sprawling unconscious on the floor. Cody stumbles er-
ratically forward.

226. TWO GUARDS ON CATWALK   (SHOOTING PAST THEM DOWN
TO CODY)
One guard raises his rifle, brings it to aim on Cody stag-
gering toward entrance. Second guard stays his fire.
Whistles are heard, blowing frantically.

227. FOLLOW SHOT ON CODY
making his erratic way toward door. The prisoners watch
in transfixed silence. Two more guards, moving carefully, close in on Cody. One guard grasps his arm, which
Cody flings off, as the other guard's arms encircle him.

They grapple, go down, struggling. In background, more guards pour through the door. On the floor, Cody, with a superhuman effort, frees himself from the guard's grip, rises again. He sees a phalanx of guards moving toward him inexorably. He backs slowly toward wall, hands outstretched in a clawlike gesture, ready to strike and tear.

A GUARD:
Come on now, Jarrett. Calm down. No sense making trouble.

The guards are closing in from all sides.

228.   CLOSE ON CODY
He is helpless, his back against the wall, the rough stone tearing at the thin convict blouse. He presses back as if he would thrust himself through the wall to freedom.

CODY:
Gotta get out . . . Gotta get out.

229.   HIGH ANGLE   NEAR WALL
the guards close in, are only a few feet from Cody. Suddenly all fight is gone out of Cody, leaving a trembling, abject figure. He slips to his knees, sobbing, fists jammed to cheeks.

CODY (sobbing):
Gotta get out . . . gotta get out.

Guards move in, until their backs obscure him.[22]
DISSOLVE TO:

230.   INT. PRISON DISPENSARY   DAY
The prison doctor is at his desk, completing a report. A guard stands at the door of the barred isolation cell. A knock is heard on entrance door, and guard goes to it, sees it is Ryley waiting outside, admits him. Ryley carries a tray of food.

RYLEY:
>   For Jarrett.

Guard leads him to isolation cell, unlocks barred door to admit Ryley. Guard closes door behind Ryley, peers in at them.

231. INT. ISOLATION CELL
A bare, bleak room. Cody, in a straitjacket, lies on a cot staring blankly at ceiling.

RYLEY:
>   Hi, Cody. Brought you some grub. Hot soup—made special.

CODY (babbling):
>   That you, Vic? Good to see ya, kid. You're okay.

RYLEY: (uneasily):
>   It's me, Cody. Tommy Ryley.

CODY:
>   That's right, Vic. Play it smart. Only way it'll work.

Ryley looks at guard, shrugs, turns back to Cody, offering him a spoonful of soup.

RYLEY:
>   Here—get some of this into ya.

232. CLOSE-UP   CODY
with spoon tipped in shot.

CODY (almost inaudibly):
>   Next time bring the gun . . .

233. CLOSE-UP—RYLEY

RYLEY (startled):
>   Huh?

234.   CODY AND RYLEY

CODY (soundlessly):
Bring the gun . . .

Ryley looks around anxiously at guard, who doesn't seem to have heard. He leans down to Cody again, holding the spoon to his lips.

RYLEY (for guard's benefit):
Sure you won't try some of this delicious soup? (A whisper.) I'll get it, Cody, if ya take me along.

CODY (loudly):
I don't want any of that slop. Try it on the warden. (Whisper.) It's a deal.

RYLEY (normal voice):
If ya don't want it I guess ya don't want it. But ya oughta keep your strength up, fella. (He winks conspiratorially at Cody and goes to the door.)

CODY (putting it on):
And if the warden don't like it try it on the governor!

RYLEY (to guard):
Guess he ain't hungry.

Guard opens the door and Ryley goes out.[23]

235.   INT. PRISON DISPENSARY
As guard leads Ryley to main door and lets him out, locking it after him, phone rings on doctor's desk. Doctor puts down pen and answers phone.

DOCTOR (into phone):
Doctor speaking . . . Yes, Warden, I've just finished my report on him . . . Violent. Homicidal. He'll probably have recurring periods of normal behavior, but I'm sure when the psychiatrists come to-

night they'll commit him to an institution for the insane . . .

DISSOLVE TO:

236.   INT. POLICE BASEMENT GARAGE   DAY
Three cars are parked together in readiness: a nondescript sedan (getaway car) and two official cars with radar-type antennas mounted on their tops. Trent, Donovan, Clark, and three uniformed police are waiting. As Trent looks at his watch, Evans emerges from elevator.

EVANS:
Oscillator all ready, Ernie?

TRENT:
Ready to sing away.

EVANS:
You park the getaway car in the trees. We'll pick you up there and take our positions.

As they pile into the cars the clocker hurries up.

CLOCKER:
Phone, Mr. Evans. Important.

Frowning, Evans gets out of car. The other cars wait.

237.   AT CLOCKER'S PHONE

EVANS (into phone):
Evans speaking . . . Oh, hello, Warden. (Listens, reacts.) Yes, it *is* bad news, but it isn't altogether a surprise . . . Thanks for your cooperation anyway, Warden . . . By the way, tomorrow there'll be a pardon coming through for one of your inmates. Vic Pardo. Rush it through, will you? . . . Thanks. (He comes grimly away from phone.)

238.   AT CARS
The men can tell from Evans's expression that a change in plan has occurred.

EVANS:
> No dice, boys. Party's off. Jarrett's a raving maniac. They've got him in a straitjacket.

TRENT:
> Good thing for Hank it happened inside the prison instead of out.

EVANS:
> That's the only good thing about it. Ernie, take the oscillator off the car. I'll get our tickets for the ten o'clock plane tonight. (To a policeman.) Could you have a car at the hotel to take us to the Springfield airport?

POLICE OFFICER:
> It'll be there, Mr. Evans.

EVANS:
> Sorry, boys. They can't all work out.[24]

>> DISSOLVE TO:

239. EXT. PENITENTIARY   LONG SHOT   NIGHT
There is a heavy fog, through which lights of main building can barely be seen.

>> DISSOLVE THROUGH TO:

240. INT. PRISON DISPENSARY   PAN SHOT   GUARD   NIGHT
as he moves from isolation cell to answer knock on door. He opens it to admit Ryley, carrying tray of food. They start toward isolation cell.

241. INT. ISOLATION CELL
Cody, in straitjacket, is being examined by two psychiatrists with prison doctor in attendance. The psychiatrists are sympathetic with Cody, who responds cooperatively. One psychiatrist, exactly Cody's physical size, wears the suit that Cody will wear in the later sequences when he kills Big Ed.

139

FIRST PSYCHIATRIST:
How would you like a change of scenery, Cody?
Someplace where we might be able to cure your
headaches? You wouldn't mind a little trip, would
you?

Ryley appears at barred door with guard. Cody gives
Ryley a quick look.

CODY:
I been thinkin' a trip might do me some good.

RYLEY:
Doctor . . . (Indicates tray.)

DOCTOR:
Not now, Ryley.

CODY (quickly):
I want my grub.

DOCTOR:
You've sent away two meals already.

CODY:
That's why I'm hungry now.

SECOND PSYCHIATRIST (patronizingly):
A good enough reason, Doctor. Hunger is always a
hopeful sign.

At a nod from the doctor, the guard unlocks the door
and comes in with Ryley, who puts the tray down beside Cody and offers him a spoon of soup. Another look
between them. Then Cody backs his head away.

CODY (harshly):
No one feeds Cody Jarrett. What am I, a kid?

PSYCHIATRIST (understandingly):
It's all right to remove the straitjacket, Doctor.

The doctor hesitates, then looks warningly at the guard,
who grips his club. Ryley moves in swiftly behind Cody.

RYLEY:

>I'll do it, sir. (He busies himself with the rear laces of the straitjacket. We do not see what he is doing, but he seems to be having difficulty.) They sure buttoned you up good . . .

Cody's arms fall limp in the sleeves of the straitjacket, his hands, of course, concealed. Second psychiatrist steps forward to pull jacket off from front. He gives a firm yank, and the sleeves unpeel from Cody's arms. It is then seen that *Cody's right hand holds a revolver.* The others' hands go up.

CODY:

>Examination's over. (Indicates guard.) Get his club, Tommy. Keep 'em quiet. (As Tommy obeys; to doctor.) Doc, you come with me. (He menaces doctor out of cell.)

242.　INT. DISPENSARY　MOVING　CODY AND DOCTOR
Cody propels the doctor toward phone on desk.

CODY:

>I want ya to make a little phone call for me. And no slipups, or *you're* gonna need a doctor.

>>>>DISSOLVE TO:

243.　INT. CELL　　　　　　　　　　　NIGHT
Vic and the Reader are lying down, reading. Guard opens the cell door.

GUARD:

>You're taking a little walk, boys. Doc wants you in the dispensary. (He leads the puzzled pair out of the cell.)

244.　CELLBLOCK
The guard leads them along to another cell, halts, opens cell door.

GUARD:
> Come on, Parker.

PARKER:
> Where to?

GUARD:
> Dispensary. Special invitation of the doctor.

Parker joins Vic and the Reader. Vic's puzzlement mounts. As the guard leads them off

DISSOLVE TO:

245.   INT. PRISON DISPENSARY   NIGHT
The room is empty, save for Ryley standing near door. Footsteps sound outside. Ryley tenses. The guard appears, preceded by Vic, Parker, and the Reader.

GUARD:
> Doc asked for these guys.

Ryley admits them. As guard steps in front of him Ryley brings club down sharply across back of guard's head, felling him.

RYLEY:
> All right, Cody.

246.   AT ISOLATION CELL
We see the prison doctor and guard securely trussed up and gagged. Cody, gun in hand, motions the two psychiatrists out of cell, trembling, hands upraised.

CODY:
> You know how jittery I am, boys. Any sudden move and I'm liable to explode.

Pan Cody and psychiatrists out into dispensary. Vic and Reader stare. Parker trembles.

READER:
> What's up, Cody?

CODY:
　What's it look like, stupid?

VIC (mind racing):
　We haven't a chance this way. We'll never get near
　the wall.

CODY:
　Who said so? Here's our plan. (Indicates captives.)

PARKER:
　Why me, Cody? What d'ya want with me?

CODY:
　I never forget a pal. I'm gonna take ya with me.
　Reader, get the straitjacket.

Reader goes into cell.

PARKER:
　Ya got it wrong, Cody! I got nothin' against ya! It
　was Big Ed told me to do it! Just give me a chance!
　(Sees no pity.) Ya wouldn't kill me in cold blood?

CODY:
　Uh-uh. I'll let ya warm up a little. (To lookout Ry-
　ley.) How is it, Tommy?

RYLEY:
　Clear as the fingerprint that nailed me.

Vic has been thinking desperately of a means of break-
ing up the attempt. He can do little. Cody faces him
with a gun. Ryley is behind him with a club. The Reader
reappears with straitjacket.

VIC:
　This don't look so hot, Cody. My way there wouldn't
　have been any shooting.

CODY:
　There ain't gonna be any my way. We're goin' out
　in a car, like gentlemen. A picnic. (To psychiatrists.)

143

Ya said ya wanted me to take a little trip. So we're goin' on a little trip. Only it better be nice and quiet.

He motions them out. Ryley opens door to corridor. Parker tries to hang back. Cody turns his gun on him. Parker, shaking, edges out. Cody and Vic follow.

DISSOLVE TO:

247. COURTYARD OUTSIDE PRISON HOSPITAL (FOG) NIGHT
The group approaches a large sedan near hospital entrance. No guards are in sight. The fog swirls around them. When they reach the sedan:

CODY (to one psychiatrist):
You're drivin'. (To other.) You get in back. (Points to straitjacket.) Reader, slip on that zootsuit and sit in the back with our friend. Make like you're loony. Vic, on the floor in back. (Turns to Ryley, indicates Parker.) Put him in the trunk.

Parker, trembling, is led by Ryley to the back of the car. Ryley opens the trunk. Parker mumbles in incoherent terror. Ryley bundles him into the trunk, slams it closed, goes around to the side of the car.

248. SIDE ANGLE OF CAR
Ryley gets in the back seat and huddles on the floor with Vic. Cody gets in beside the psychiatrist at wheel and crouches under dashboard.

249. SHOT OF GUARD PATROLLING YARD
He peers into the almost impenetrable fog as he hears car doors shut and starts toward the source of the sound.

250. INT. CAR
The psychiatrist is fumbling in his pockets.

CODY:
Get goin'. Out the way ya came in.

144

PSYCHIATRIST:
> The keys—I forgot the keys! (For a moment it seems that Cody will kill the man.) You wouldn't let me bring my coat. They're in my coat.

CODY (controls himself):
> That won't stop us. (He leans under steering column.)

251.   DOLLY SHOT—GUARD
coming closer, peering ahead, alert.

252.   INT. CAR
Cody, *hands unseen*, jerks the two wires from the switch, hooks them together.

CODY:
> Press the starter.

The psychiatrist obeys. The motor turns over, then dies. Again the starter. The motor starts.

253.   EXT. CAR
Guard reaches it as it starts moving. He catches a glimpse of the driver as car goes out of shot, recognizes him.

GUARD:
> Good night, sir.

254.   REAR GATE OF PENITENTIARY
The car stops at the gate. Another guard appears from watchhouse, shines a flashlight on driver's face.

GUARD:
> Rough night to be out, Doctor.

He opens the gate and the car drives out. Barely has the guard closed the gate after it than the sirens begin to scream from the tower.

DISSOLVE TO:

256.   INT. POLICE CAR   (PROCESS)   NIGHT
Police officer driving, Evans beside him; in back, Donovan, Clark, and Trent, with wrapped oscillator on his
lap. Treasury men have briefcases, etc. Phone indicator
flashes on dashboard. Given the okay by driver, Evans
picks it up.

EVANS (into phone):
Hello . . . Speaking . . . What . . . ! Right away. (To
driver.) Turn back! Jarrett's busted out!

256.   FULL SHOT   CAR   NIGHT
It makes a screaming U-turn. Siren and red lights are
switched instantly.

257.   INT. POLICE CAR   (PROCESS)   NIGHT
Police lieutenant and Donovan in front, Evans and Trent
in back, listening to police broadcast. Car speeds, siren
sounding.

POLICE ANNOUNCER'S VOICE:
. . . Black sedan—license six-X-four-three-zero—
probably headed southwest. Hold it. Here are the
names of the men who escaped with Jarrett. Thomas
Ryley, Roy Parker, Michael Curtin, Vic Pardo . . .
Descriptions later. Attention. Do not shoot unless
absolutely necessary. Hostages in car. Do not shoot
unless absolutely necessary. Hostages in car.

EVANS (grimly):
One break for our boy.

TRENT:
What's Hank's procedure now?

EVANS:
He'll stay with Jarrett till he gets what he's after—

POLICE ANNOUNCER'S VOICE:
Descriptions follow: Cody Jarrett, five nine, one

hundred sixty pounds, brown hair, prison uniform, etc.

DISSOLVE TO:

258.   INT. FARMHOUSE   MED. CLOSE   CODY   NIGHT
He stands before a mirror, buttoning a trim dark suit, which he has taken from one of the psychiatrists, who will be revealed dressed in Cody's prison suit. Draw back to show a farmhouse living room. The two psychiatrists are seated on two chairs, gagged, back to back; the Reader is tying them fast. The owners of the house, an aged farmer and his wife, are covered against a wall by Ryley. Both Ryley and the Reader have changed into ill-fitting clothes. Cody turns from mirror, picks up his revolver.

CODY (adjusting suit; to psychiatrists):
   I like your tailor. How do you like mine? (To Ryley.)
   Get some grub, Tommy.

Ryley exits toward kitchen hallway seen in background.

CODY (calling):
   What's takin' ya so long, Vic?

259.   INT. HALLWAY   CLOSE   VIC

VIC:
   Tryin' to rustle up some guns.

Vic, who has also changed, is rustling through a closet, pretending to look for guns. He turns, sees phone on wall, heads stealthily for it, edging along wall. He reaches his hand toward phone, just as it starts to ring. He is stymied, perhaps in danger. In the moment of his hesitation:

CODY'S VOICE:
   Let it ring!

260.   WIDER ANGLE   CODY AND VIC
Cody has appeared in hallway. Vic is at phone, but Cody's

conclusion is that he was going to answer it. The phone continues to ring.

VIC:
> Someone might get suspicious.

CODY (yanks phone off wall):
> So they're at a movie. Come on. (Into living room.) Hey!

They go to the front door, followed by Ryley (with a bag of food) and the Reader.[25]

261.   EXT. FARMHOUSE   NIGHT
lonely as all farmhouses. As the fugitives come outside Cody takes a chicken leg from the bag of food. A station wagon is parked by the psychiatrist's limousine. Cody raps on limousine trunk.

CODY:
> How ya doin', Parker? (Parker's voice is heard, muffled, unintelligible.) Stuffy, huh? (Fires three times into car's trunk; to others.) Air.[26]

Still munching at his chicken leg, Cody gets into the station wagon with the others and drives away.

                                        DISSOLVE TO:

262.   EXT. LODGE HOUSE   LONG SHOT   NIGHT
Black night. Low moaning wind in the trees. One room lighted downstairs. Though house is probably on Lake Arrowhead shore, tonight it might be a million miles from anywhere. It has the eerie look of a house of fear.

                               DISSOLVE THROUGH TO:

263.   INT. LODGE HOUSE LIVING ROOM   CLOSE ON RADIO
                                                NIGHT
From it emerges:

ANNOUNCER'S VOICE:
> . . . No clue to their movements has been reported since their assault last night on a motorist north of

Gallup, New Mexico. It is assumed now by federal law-enforcement agencies that Jarrett and the other escaped convicts are heading for a hideout in California. This concludes the nightly news summary from KFKL, the Voice of San Bernardino. When you hear the tone the time—

During this camera has drawn back to show Verna listening nervously by the fireplace. She switches off the radio. The room is big, comfortable. Stairway leads to second floor. Curtains are drawn. When the radio stops, Verna reacts, turns, at the sound of a small bell jingling.

264.   LOW   CLOSE ANGLE AT DOOR
to reveal a warning device in the form of a bell attached to wall beside front door, a few inches above floor. A thread attached to bell stretches across the width of door, is fastened to wall on opposite side. Big Ed again swings door inward so that it meets the obstruction of the thread. The bell jingles. Satisfied that no one can steal in unheard, Ed closes door.

265.   MED. FULL   LIVING ROOM
Verna sits motionless in a chair, staring into fire. Big Ed comes to her from door.

BIG ED:
    Did you check the shutters? (No answer.) I said did you—

VERNA (turns; tense):
    Ed—let's get out of here!

BIG ED (checking his guns):
    Take it easy, sugar. We're ready for him when he comes.

VERNA:
    I can't stand another night, Ed—listenin'—goin' crazy. It isn't like just waitin' for some human being

149

who wants to kill ya. Cody ain't human. Fill him full of lead and he'll still come at ya.

BIG ED:
If he's plugged he falls. Like anybody else.

VERNA:
The boys didn't think so. Why did they beat it down to San Berdoo?

BIG ED:
Because this is between me and Cody. They'll be back when it's settled.

VERNA (lifelessly):
You'll be dead.

BIG ED (slowly):
Maybe. But the time comes when a man's gotta stop runnin' away and face it out. Or keep runnin' for good.

VERNA:
All right! Throw your life away! Stay here and shoot it out. Me? I'm goin'. I wanta live. (Starts upstairs.)

BIG ED:
Cody'll have a few ideas about that.

VERNA:
I'll go someplace he'll never find me.

BIG ED (softly):
The world ain't big enough, sugar—not when he knows what you did to his ma.

VERNA (halts; gasps):
You'd tell him?

BIG ED:
If you run out on me, why not?

VERNA:
I only did it for you, Ed. She had you covered.

BIG ED:
> Cody still won't like hearing she got it in the back.
> (She stares, terrified.) Feel more like staying now?

VERNA (beaten):
> Yeah.

BIG ED:
> So we wait. You and me. Till we know the answer.
> Tonight—tomorrow—whenever he comes. It'll be me
> or Cody.

She goes slowly upstairs, barely able to support herself.

266. INT. VERNA'S BEDROOM   CLOSE ON VERNA   NIGHT
Verna lies awake, in terror. The shutters creak. A bird
caws. Finally, Verna can stand it no longer. She gets out
of bed, begins to slip out of her nightgown.

DISSOLVE TO:

267. INT. ON STAIRWAY   CLOSE ON VERNA'S FEET   NIGHT
Verna's legs are seen stealthily descending the stairs.
Every step is dangerous. When she has reached the bot-
tom, truck with her to front door. Her hands dips into
shot, carefully holds bell so that it won't ring. The door
opens, she edge through it, still holding the bell. Only
her hand is seen now as, cautiously, it releases the bell.
No sound. Her hand disappears. The door closes softly.

268. EXT. HOUSE   PAN SHOT   VERNA   NIGHT
A wind sighs around her as she hurries toward open
garage.

269. EXT. GARAGE
The moon makes a tracery of shadows on the ground.
Verna, heart racing, comes into shot. Suddenly, there is
a sound as of a footstep. Verna stiffens, a scream ready
on her lips. She stares about wildly at the dancing shadows made by the swaying trees, each shadow a poten-
tial enemy, each, sudden death. She looks up.

270.   ROOF OF GARAGE   (VERNA'S ANGLE)
An overhanging branch moves in the wind, brushes
against the wooden roof, making the sound heard before.

271.   VERNA   (TRUCKING)
relieved, almost sobbing, moves toward car in garage.
As she reaches the door camera halts abruptly as she
runs into the grasping arms of Cody Jarrett, who steps
out of the blackness to intercept her. (NOTE: This camera
movement should have the effect of a body blow delivered suddenly and without warning.) His hand stifles
her scream. Her eyes dilate in terror. Cody is cat with
mouse.

CODY:
Not expectin' me, huh? How come, honey? I told ya
I'd be back. (Moves hand from her mouth.) Now tell
me you're glad to see me—but say it soft so we won't
wake up nobody.

VERNA (the pitch of her life):
Oh, Cody, I'm so glad to see ya. I been prayin' ya'd
come back. I couldn't stand it any longer. I was runnin' away . . .

CODY:
From Big Ed?

VERNA:
Yeah.

CODY (too gently):
Why? Don't ya like him?

VERNA:
No . . . No . . .

CODY:
Maybe ya shouldn't've teamed up with him in the
first place.

VERNA:

> I couldn't help it, Cody! He said if I didn't go with him he'd have ya killed! I couldn't stand that!

CODY (grins):

> You're good, Verna. The way you can turn it on.

VERNA:

> All I wanted was for ya to come back! That's the truth! I love ya, Cody! I love ya!

CODY (fiercely):

> Ya let Ma die!

VERNA:

> No!

CODY (slaps her):

> Didn't raise a finger! Just stood there and watched Big Ed kill her!

VERNA:

> Ya got it wrong, Cody! I swear!

CODY (slaps her again):

> Maybe ya laughed about it later? An old woman tryin' to stand up to a guy like that!

VERNA:

> I tell ya, ya got it all wrong! I tried to warn her—but he caught me and beat me. And then when Ma came he was waitin' for her and he—he—(Sobs.) Oh, I can't tell ya, Cody!

CODY:

> Tell me . . .

VERNA (low):

> He got her in the back. (Cody takes a deep breath.) You gotta be careful, Cody! He's got the house all rigged like a trap. Ya can't get in unless I tell you how.

CODY:
  I'm waitin'.

DISSOLVE TO:

272.   INT. BEDROOM   MED. SHOT   BED   NIGHT
The room is in almost pitch darkness. In bed is a figure
huddled as though in sleep. The tinkling of the alarm
bell downstairs is heard.
  Draw back swiftly to show Big Ed tensing in a chair,
cocking his revolver. He moves silently to the bed, rear-
ranges the pillows beneath the covers so that they look
more like a man sleeping, then tiptoes back to a vantage
point commanding the door. He lifts his revolver. A slight
creaking of stairs is heard. Big Ed's finger readies on the
trigger. The door handle turns, the door opens a couple
of inches.

VERNA'S VOICE (softly):
  Ed . . . Ed . . .

As she enters room, reaches for the "figure" in bed:

BIG ED:
  Stay where you are!

VERNA (swinging around; startled):
  Ed!

BIG ED:
  What was that bell?

VERNA (under a strain):
  It was me, Ed.

BIG ED:
  What were you doing?

VERNA:
  I couldn't go through with it. I tried and I couldn't!

BIG ED:
  Make sense.

154

VERNA (it is wrung from her):
> I was gonna take the car and beat it. I was scared.
> But I don't wanta go anymore.

During this, Big Ed has come closer to her, off-guard.

273. CLOSE   BIG ED AND VERNA
Half-opened door in background, Big Ed's back to door.
He puts his arms around her, tightly. His revolver muzzle
is hard against her back.

VERNA (as though in pain):
> Ed . . . the gun . . .

He tosses gun onto bed, crushes her to him. Releasing
her he sees the strain in her face.

BIG ED:
> Still got nerves?

VERNA (nodding):
> I'd like a drink. Please—Ed . . .

She maneuvers out of his arms, goes to bureau on which
stands a bottle and some glasses. Ed moves over near
door to hallway, snaps light switch. As light comes on
and Ed turns:[27]

274. FULL SHOT   CODY
In open doorway of connecting door to another bedroom. His face is deadly, his gun raised.[28]

275. BIG ED
Fear in his eyes. He acts instinctively, knowing his death
is at hand. He wheels, races through the door to hallway. Verna waits, frozen.

276. FLASH SHOT ON CODY
as he pulls trigger. Gun flames twice.

155

277.   DOOR
as Big Ed, hit, stumbles through door, slamming it shut behind him. Cody comes swiftly into shot, his gun spitting death through the door.

278.   UPPER HALLWAY   NEAR STAIRS   PANNING SHOT
as Big Ed, fatally wounded, stumbles with his last bit of strength toward the head of the stairs. He falls, tumbling heavily down them, camera panning.

279.   BIG ED AT FOOT OF STAIRS
He lies there in a twisted position—dead.

280.   HEAD OF STAIRS
as Cody comes in and stares down at Big Ed's lifeless body. Slowly Verna comes in and stands beside him, almost afraid to look down at what she knows she will see.

281.   REVERSE ANGLE   SHOOTING PAST CODY TO INCLUDE FRONT DOOR
through which Vic, Ryley, and Reader now drift. They look at Big Ed's body, then up at Cody.

282.   CLOSE ON CODY
His expression, as he returns their look, tells them: "That's what happens to anyone who crosses Cody Jarrett."

FADE OUT[29]
FADE IN

283.   INT. LODGE HOUSE   FULL SHOT   DAY
Cody, Vic, the Reader, Ryley, Cotton, Happy, and Het Kohler are seated around a table, poring over the detailed layout of a factory, which Cotton, Het, and Happy use to illustrate a heist planned by the late Ed Somers.

HAPPY:
Ed said the joint was a cinch for fifty grand.

CODY:
So far it smells. But what did ya expect from Big Ed?
Go on.

HET:
Well, the way he had it figured, we pile outa the
cars here—slug the guards—grab the payroll here—
and blast our way out. Take fifty seconds.

RYLEY:
They got cars and they follow ya.

COTTON:
That's where we use the gas truck, Cody. I stall it
right in the gates. When we beat it in the getaway
cars, I got the truck keys in my pocket.

CODY:
Where do ya get a gas truck?

HET:
We got one stashed in the trees. Bought it with our
own dough. Twelve grand.

CODY:
You bought a gas truck! Have you forgotten how to
steal one?

READER:
Maybe it ain't so bad, Cody. Twelve grand and ya
get fifty.

CODY:
Fence it and ya wind up with twenty. What're ya
gonna do with that— buy a couple more trucks?

VIC (carefully):
A joint like that's got the serial number of every bill.
Any guy says he can fence fifty grand of it's crazy.

HAPPY:
The Trader ain't crazy.

VIC:

> The Trader?

CODY:

> My manager, kid. (Vic conceals his excitement.) Let's take a look at this twelve-grand jalopy.

As they start out Verna emerges from her room upstairs.

VERNA:

> Oh, Cody—my radio ain't workin' again.

CODY:

> So what do ya want for it—unemployment insurance?

VERNA (petulantly):

> Can't I run down to San Berdoo and get it fixed?

CODY:

> Nobody moves outa here until I say so! Go back to bed and read your comic books.

She returns to her room. The others have exited, but Vic has lingered behind and goes outside with Cody.

284.   EXT. LODGE HOUSE   MOVING SHOT   VIC AND CODY
tagging behind the rest of the mob.

VIC:

> This guy ya call the Trader. Can ya trust him?

CODY:

> Why?

VIC (shrugging):

> I wouldn't like my share of any caper bein' handed to some guy might disappear with it.

CODY (grinning):

> Suspicious, ain't ya?

VIC:

> Just careful.

CODY:
>Ya don't have to worry about the Trader. Pays off on the spot. Nice clean bills.

VIC:
>How does he get rid of the stuff?

CODY:
>Ships over to Europe. Collects both ends.

VIC:
>Smart operator, huh?

CODY:
>Ya didn't see any bills from the tunnel job poppin' up, did ya?

VIC (a grin):
>Uh-uh, I like him better now.

285.   EXT. FULL SHOT   GASOLINE TRUCK   DAY
as they reach the fringe of trees, where Het yanks off a tarpaulin to reveal gasoline truck—a huge, shining fourteen-wheeler. The Reader and Tommy Ryley swarm over it, examining everything with childlike curiosity. Even Vic and Cody are impressed. Het, Happy, and Cotton await Cody's verdict eagerly.

CODY (studying truck thoughtfully):
>Hey—not bad. Maybe your twelve grand don't go down the drain after all. (Opens storage-compartment door.) Say, Het—you're quite a guy with a blowtorch. Could ya cut a hole from in here up into the tank?

HET:
>Easy.

Cody dances a little high-spirited jig.

CODY:
>We're back in business, boys. But not Big Ed's way. And not for any fifty G's. First a question. Say ya

wanted to push in a joint like Fort Knox and grab a coupla tons of gold— What's the toughest thing in a job like that?

RYLEY:
Gettin' inside the joint.

CODY:
A silver dollar for the gentleman in the balcony. Right on the button. Gettin' in. And that brings me to a little story Ma used to tell me when I was a kid. A story about a horse. (Cotton and Het look at each other blankly.) 'Way back there was a whole army tryin' to knock over a place called Troy and gettin' nowhere fast. Couldn't put a dent in the walls. Then one morning the people in Troy wake up and look over the walls—and the army's taken a powder. Men, boats, the works. Just one thing they left behind: a big wooden horse. (Licks his lips.) Well, according' to Ma . . .

DISSOLVE TO:

286.   EXT. GASOLINE TRUCK
A beehive of activity. Cotton is painting a stencil on the side of the driver's cab: Capacity 18,000 lbs. Happy and Ryley are bent down into the innards of the motor. Het lowers a light plug attached to a length of electric cord through a hole in top of gas compartment. Reader is in driver's cab.

287.   INT. GASOLINE COMPARTMENT
Vic, using a flashlight, receives the light plug as it is lowered in by Het. He screws in a bulb, which lights up the submarinelike compartment.

VIC (calling up):
Okay—try it.

288.   EXT. GASOLINE TRUCK
as Het, hearing Vic, nods to Reader in driver's cab.

160

289.   EXT. MOVING SHOT   STATION WAGON
entering lodge grounds driven by a distinguished-looking
stranger. He is dressed for fishing, Abercrombie and Fitch
style: flies and lures in hatband, wicker creel, etc.

290.   GROUP AT TRUCK   (STATION WAGON APPROACHING IN
BACKGROUND)
The men pause warily and watch the station wagon pull
to a stop nearby. As the man gets out:

291.   INT. DRIVER'S CAB   CLOSE   READER
He blows the horn—short-long-short—then descends.

292.   GROUP AT TRUCK
The stranger saunters up to group, creel over shoulder.

STRANGER:
    Run out of gas?

The men, tense, ugly, say nothing. At this moment Vic
crawls out of the storage compartment. This is a dead
giveaway, and they know it. The stranger, however,
tactfully ignores it. He coughs gently.

STRANGER:
    I was—ah—wondering if I might use your tele-
    phone.

COTTON:
    There ain't a phone for five miles.

STRANGER:
    Oh. I'm sorry to hear that.

293.   MOVING SHOT   CODY
Summoned by the horn, he has come from the house.
As he reaches group:

CODY:
    Lost your way, mister?

161

STRANGER (turning):
> Oh, good morning. No, I wanted to call my office, but these gentlemen—

CODY:
> There's a phone inside. I'll show ya where it is.

STRANGER (looks from group to Cody):
> Why—ah—thank you very much.

He follows Cody out of shot and toward the house. The others grimly watch them go.

READER:
> There's a call that's gonna cost more'n a nickel.

HET:
> Looks like Big Ed'll have company.

RYLEY:
> And we got a new station wagon.

He elaborately puts a finger to each ear, closes his eyes, waiting for the shot.

294.   INT. LODGE HOUSE
as Cody and stranger enter, close door.

CODY:
> How's fishin'?

STRANGER:
> Fine, Cody. Good catch.

They shake hands warmly, then the stranger opens his creel and withdraws rolled blueprints.

CODY:
> Ya like the truck idea, huh?

TRADER:
> Admirable. We might *all* profit from a closer study of classical literature.

CODY (looks at blueprints):
Chemical plant. Guess that's Long Beach way.

TRADER:
That's close enough. You know the way I work, Cody.
I must ask you not to insist on knowing the exact
location until you reach the rendezvous.

CODY:
Sure, Trader, sure. There's only one thing matters—
how much has this joint got in the kitty?

TRADER:
Two hundred forty thousand dollars will be placed
in their safe before closing time tomorrow and paid
out to the deserving employees the following morning—barring an unforeseen accident, of course.

CODY:
Such as me and my boys.

TRADER:
Exactly.

295.   EXT. AT TRUCK
Ryley lowers fingers from ears. The men are puzzled.

RYLEY:
What are they doin'—dancin'?

READER:
Maybe they found they went to school together.

HET:
They might be buddies at that—

VIC:
Well, somethin' funny's goin' on.

Wipes hands on grease rag, starts off.

296. INT. LODGE HOUSE   CODY AND TRADER
Trader refastens lid of creel. Cody continues to examine blueprints.

TRADER:
I've had my eye on the place for months, Cody, but until you hit upon the Trojan horse idea there was simply no way of getting in a large enough body of men.

CODY:
These checking gates. That means a pass for the driver—identity cards and stuff. We're all hot.

TRADER:
Your truck will be driven past the checkers by an ex-convict of my acquaintance who now leads a scrupulously honest life—as a truck driver for this very firm.

CODY:
Smooth.

Vic enters.

VIC:
Sorry to bust in, Cody, but we're finished out there and I thought ya might want to check it.

CODY:
I'll be right out.

Vic goes to door, hesitates, turns.

VIC:
Havin' much luck, mister?

TRADER:
Hadn't started. I was just on my way.

VIC:
Oh. Do much fishin' up here?

TRADER:
Every year.

VIC:
What're ya after, mister?

TRADER:
Bass.

VIC (slams door shut):
Get this guy, Cody! He's a phony!

TRADER:
I beg your pardon.

VIC:
This is trout country. There ain't bass for a hundred miles. (Trader looks to Cody, who chuckles heartily.) What's so funny?

CODY:
Ya're right on your toes, kid. That's rich. (A look at Trader.) Bass! Got ya, didn't he? This is the guy I was tellin ya about. Trader—meet Vic Pardo.

VIC:
How are ya, Mister—er—

TRADER (smoothly):
Forgive me, but I keep my identity from all but the leaders of a very few select organizations.

CODY:
Forget it, Trader. Vic's my partner. Fifty-fifty.

TRADER (puzzled):
Cody Jarrett giving fifty-fifty?

CODY (rather sharply):
I split even with Ma, didn't I?

TRADER:
I see. (Extends his hand.) The name's Daniel Winston—San Diego— (With a smile.) Securities.

VIC (as they shake hands):
Glad to know ya, Mr. Winston. (He isn't kidding.)
DISSOLVE TO:

297. EXT. THE LODGE LONG SHOT NIGHT
The windows dark. A second-story window opens silently and a man begins to climb out. There is a faint crackling of a man's footsteps as camera pulls back to reveal Happy Taylor, behind a tree, watching the window. As the figure drops quietly to the ground Happy's hand goes to his shoulder holster.

298. MED. SHOT VIC
beneath the window, picks himself up. He looks around carefully, ignorant of the fact that he is being watched, creeps stealthily along the side of the house, then veers away toward the trees and the road beyond.

299. CLOSE SHOT—HAPPY TAYLOR
concealed behind the tree, revolver ready.

300. MED. FOLLOW SHOT VIC
heading through the trees, toward a road in background. Hold as from behind tree—directly into Vic's path—steps Happy Taylor, revolver aimed.

HAPPY:
Goin' someplace, Pardo?

Vic goes into action, utilizing his official jujitsu training. One arm swings Happy's gun away. In the same motion he clamps the arm in a viselike grip. The gun drops as Happy's face twists in pain. A blow to his stomach doubles him up. Another on the jaw fells him. It has all happened swiftly, silently. Vic kneels to examine the unconscious figure. A pair of legs steps into shot behind Vic, one foot kicking Happy's gun away.

CODY'S VOICE (softly):
Somethin' wrong kid?

Vic stiffens. Draw back as he rises. Cody stands a few feet away, his face hard, expressionless. He holds a gun. Vic decides offense is the best defense.

VIC (harshly):
Tell your gorillas I don't like bein' pushed around.

CODY (calm; threatening):
My orders were nobody leaves.

VIC:
That might go for hoods like him, but if I got a reason to leave, I leave.

CODY (voice hard):
Nobody's got any reasons I don't know about!

Happy stirs, sits up, retrieves his gun.

HAPPY:
He jumped me, Cody.

CODY:
Get back on the job. (Happy leaves, nursing his jaw.) Cody turns back to Vic. (Soft; menacing.) That was pretty fancy wrestlin', kid. Where'd ya learn it?

VIC:
In the army.

CODY:
You're lyin'. They don't take cons in the army.

VIC:
When the war started I didn't have any record except kid stuff.

CODY:
What were ya doin' just now, soldier, goin' over the hill?

VIC:
No. I got to thinkin' I could slip into L.A.—be back before anybody knew.

CODY:
What goes on in L.A.?

VIC:
My wife. She don't know where I am. When we
crashed out I didn't leave no forwardin' address.

CODY (after a pause):
Mmm.

VIC:
That's the truth, Cody.

CODY:
Then why didn't ya ask me?

VIC:
I figured ya'd get sore.

CODY:
So ya took off on your own.

VIC:
Been a long time since I seen her. I'm human, like
anybody else.

CODY:
All right kid, all right. You're just lonesome—like
me.

VIC:
You? What about—? (Gestures toward house.)

CODY:
Verna? (Snorts.) All I ever really had was Ma—and
now she's gone. Ya remember your mother, kid?

VIC:
She died before I even knew her.[30]

301.   CLOSE ON CODY
He seems to be staring past Vic to some distant point of
his own. His voice is low, a half-whisper.

CODY:

I just been walkin' around thinkin' of mine. Ma didn't have much. Always runnin'—always on the move. Some life. First there was the old man—died screamin' and kickin'. And after that, just takin' care of me all the time, wantin' me to be on top of the world. Times when I thought I was losin' my grip there was Ma right behind me, pushin' me back to the top again. And now what's she got to show for it?

302.   CODY AND VIC

VIC:

Well, anyway, she's quit runnin', Cody.

CODY:

Yeah . . . Ya know, kid, I'd like to stop runnin' myself sometime, but there's somethin' drivin' me— always drivin' me—in here— (Touches temple.) Won't let me alone. But just now—walkin' around out there—I was okay. Seemed there was just me and Ma. Ya know what? Thinkin' about it, it was like I was dead, too. And it was kind of a good feelin' . . . (Rejecting all this.) Aaah, maybe I *am* crazy. Let's go in and have a drink.[31]

DISSOLVE TO:

303.   INT. LODGE

Verna, in negligee, is at sideboard mixing drinks.

CODY:

Tell you what, Vic. We'll pick up your wife sometime after the job tomorrow. Maybe the four of us can take a trip . . . relax for a while.

VIC:

Sounds good to me.

VERNA (handing drink to Cody):
> You mean it, honey? We could have fun. Live big. Money's just paper if ya don't spend it.

CODY:
> It's just an idea.

VERNA:
> But it's a good idea. Europe, maybe. Paris! Rubbin' shoulders with the best of 'em. (Acting it out.) How'd'ja do, Countess . . . My hands drippin' jewels—sable on my back. I'd knock their eyes out. Ya'd be awful proud of me, Cody.

CODY:
> Don't blow your top.

VERNA (handing Vic drink):
> He ain't thought of a vacation for years. Don't let him forget it.

CODY (lifts glass):
> To us, kid. Top of the world.

Vic lifts glass. They drink. Over rim of glass, Vic thoughtfully eyes Verna. A plan formulates.

VIC (casually):
> How's the radio comin'?

VERNA:
> A crystal set'd play better.[32]

VIC:
> Maybe I could get it workin' for ya?

VERNA:
> Wish ya could, Vic. I'm dead without music.

CODY:
> Skip it. We'll get a new one.

VIC:

> I don't mind, Cody. Keep me busy. I couldn't sleep anyway.

CODY:

> Whatever ya say, kid.

VERNA (at cabinet):

> I was just gettin' ready to throw it away. (Brings portable radio to Vic.)

VIC:

> I ain't makin' any promises, remember.

CODY (to Verna):

> We better hit the hay. You're liable to catch cold in that thing. (As they start out.) See ya in the morning, Vic. (With a chuckle.) And this time keep your windows closed.[33]

Vic answers with a grin. Cody and Verna exit. Vic, a frown on his face, stares down at radio.

> DISSOLVE TO:

304. INT. VIC'S ROOM   CLOSE ON RADIO   NIGHT
Revealing the inner mechanism. Vic's hands work swiftly, remove the transformer. Pull back to show that he has already taken out two tubes and detached some wires. Also extracts two extra "B" batteries from storage space. Skillfully, he attaches these odd pieces to each other, wires them, tests them by touching two wires to each other. A buzzing sound is heard as the circuit is closed.

> DISSOLVE TO:

305. EXT. LODGE   FULL SHOT   DAY
scurrying activity. The truck has been brought out into the open. A black sedan is parked behind it. The men are passing small boxes, weapons, ammunition, flashlights, and blowtorch equipment in through the storage compartment. Vic is lying beneath the rear axle of truck,

apparently attaching an antistatic chain. Cody and Verna
come from house. Cody pauses at rear of truck.

CODY:
> What ya doin', kid? We're on our way.

306. CLOSE VIC BENEATH TRUCK AXLE
He is attaching chain. Cody's legs visible in shot.

VIC:
> Gotta have a chain bounce on the ground—get rid
> of electricity.

CODY'S VOICE:
> That's only when ya got gas or chemicals sloppin'
> around inside.

VIC:
> Ya want some traffic cop to think we got a load of
> somethin' else?

CODY'S VOICE:
> That's usin' your head. But snap it up. (His feet move
> away as he begins final instructions.) Now ya've all
> been told what to do.

During this Vic puts chain aside and busies himself fur-
tively with something else.

307. INSERT RADIO OSCILLATOR
Vic's hands, working on oscillator he has fashioned from
parts of portable radio, swiftly connect a wire running
from the motor's generator to a terminal.

308. MED. FULL GROUP
Vic emerges from under rear of truck. Verna is at wheel
of sedan. During the foregoing Cody has continued with
his instructions.

CODY:
> Ya know where the rendezvous is. We pick up our

driver there at five o'clock so we get to the plant right after the day shift's checked off. Vic—Tommy— we ride to the rendezvous in the truck. The rest of ya go with Verna in the sedan. Make your own time, but be there.

As everyone piles into the two vehicles

DISSOLVE TO:

309. EXT. HIGHWAY   FULL SHOT   DAY
The truck rolling down the highway, Ryley driving, Cody and Vic beside him in cab.

310. CLOSE SHOT (MOVING) ON RADIATOR OF TRUCK   DAY
Steam starts to spiral out of radiator. Pan up to shoot through windshield. A look of grim satisfaction crosses Vic's face briefly as he pretends not to notice. Cody frowns.

CODY:
Twelve thousand bucks and this tin can makes tea.

VIC:
We better get water. A cracked radiator won't get us where we're goin'.

RYLEY:
Gas station down the hill, Cody.

CODY (after a moment):
Pull in. Watch yourself.

DISSOLVE TO:

311. EXT. GAS STATION
An elderly, beaming man approaches the truck.

ATTENDANT:
Fill 'er up?

CODY:
With water, bub. Check the radiator.

Seeing the look, attendant goes to front of truck, lifts

hood, peers in. Vic watches stonily, from a cab which is
tipped in background.

ATTENDANT:
Dry as a bone. Someone left the valve open.

312.   VIC AND CODY
By no sign does Vic's face indicate that this is what he
knew the attendant would find.

ATTENDANT'S VOICE:
Be just a minute while I give her a long drink.

VIC:
You got a washroom, bud?

313.   FULL SHOT

ATTENDANT (points; proudly):
Cleanest in the West.

He starts to hose radiator as Vic climbs down from truck
and starts toward rear of gas station where a small
wooden frame building stands with a white lettered sign
above it: Washroom—Cleanest in the West.
                                    QUICK DISSOLVE TO:

314.   CLOSE ON RADIATOR
as water comes up to top. Attendant's hand turns off the
hose, withdraws it, replaces radiator cap. Draw back to
wide angle.

ATTENDANT:
There you are. Good as new.

CODY (to Ryley):
Get Vic.

315.   INT. WASHROOM   VIC
He is looking frantically for something, finally finds it
in a locker—a bar of cleaning soap. At the wash basin
he moistens soap and with it writes on mirror: Police—

Call Evans Treasury—Radio Signal—Fallon. He hears
footsteps, swiftly divests himself of jacket, hangs it from
light bracket over mirror, obscuring message. Door opens.

RYLEY:
Cody's gettin' anxious.

VIC:
Be right there.

Ryley exits. Vic gets his coat, exits.

316. AT TRUCK
Attendant is wiping off the windshield. Cody waits impatiently. Ryley comes in, followed by Vic. They climb
into truck.

VIC:
I thought you said cleanest in the West?

ATTENDANT:
You ever seen one cleaner, mister?

VIC:
The mirror's so dirty ya see double.

The truck moves off out of shot, leaving the attendant
glaring after them angrily.

ATTENDANT:
Wise guys. Didn't even buy gas.

He looks speculatively off at washroom for an instant,
then shrugs and goes about his business.

DISSOLVE TO:

317. EXT. REAR OF SMALL ROADHOUSE   LATER AFTERNOON
This is a small roadhouse off the main highway. Verna
and the members of mob are standing by sedan, smoking. The gas truck swings in from highway, comes around
the rear where group is waiting. It stops. Cody, Ryley,
and Vic alight.

CODY:

> Wait here. (He goes off toward rear door of road-house.)

318. MED. SHOT TRADER

He materializes in doorway as Cody enters shot.

CODY:

> Where do we go, Trader?

Trader hands folded piece of paper to Cody, who glances at it, whistles appreciatively.

CODY:

> We'll be here. Where's the driver?

TRADER:

> Having a drink. He'll be right out.

CODY (calls off):

> Into the wooden horse, boys.

319. AT TRUCK

as the men climb in, Vic among them.

320. AT DOOR OF ROADHOUSE

The driver comes out. *He is Bo Creel.*

CODY:

> Well, Bo! I heard you were on the straight and narrow, drivin' a truck for a livin'.

BO CREEL (grins):

> Tonight I hand in my resignation.

TRADER:

> You'd better get started, Cody. Good luck.

Cody nods, starts off with Bo, camera panning.

CODY:
> There's a button up front. Press it once if trouble shows. Three or four times for all clear.

BO CREEL:
> I get ya.

They pause as Cody reaches Verna by sedan, shows her paper.

CODY:
> Park outside—across the street. Anything goes wrong, lean on the horn.

Verna gets into sedan, drives off.

321. AT TRUCK
The last man is disappearing inside. Cody comes up. Bo Creel climbs into driver's cab.

CODY (calling inside):
> How's it in there?

HET'S VOICE:
> Can't breathe good—otherwise fine.

CODY (grinning):
> Who says we gotta breathe? (He climbs inside, closes door after him.)

322. FULL SHOT
The Trader nods to Bo. Truck moves off.

> DISSOLVE TO:

323. EXT. GAS STATION   LATE AFTERNOON
The Attendant is giving a customer his change. Another man comes in, gets into car beside driver.

MAN:
> Somebody's ribbing you, Russ. Take a squint in the mirror.

177

Car drives off. Attendant looks at washroom, then starts
back toward it, picking up a bucket and damp rag.

DISSOLVE TO:

324.   INT. EVANS'S OFFICE   LATE AFTERNOON
Evans, in his shirt-sleeves, is on the phone, face taut
with excitement. Ernie Trent hovers anxiously nearby.

EVANS (into phone):
    You bet I know what it means! (To Ernie). It's Hank!
    (Back to phone.) Call the FCC. Get every range-
    finding car they've got—ask them to clear the air.
    Now, listen . . .

During this he has risen to his feet and is already slip-
ping on his shoulder holster, as we

DISSOLVE TO:

325.   FLASH SHORT (IN MONTAGE EFFECT)   LATE AFTERNOON
    1. Agent's car (FCC), its square shortwave direction-
finder antenna turning slowly.
    2. A second car (FCC) interior, the driver with head-
phones, the man beside him controlling the range
finder—like a submarine periscope being operated from
below.
    3. A third car (FCC), direction-finder equipped, con-
taining anxious Evans and Trent in back seat behind
driver and operator. Evans wears headphones.

DISSOLVE TO:

326.   EXT. HIGHWAY   LATE AFTERNOON
The truck coming down the highway.

327.   INT. GAS TRUCK   MED. CLOSE
The men crouched in the dim light from single bulb,
much like men in single compartment of submarine.
Cody has a blueprint spread out in front of him.

CODY:
    That's it. Everyone straight on what he's supposed
    to do?

They ad-lib "Yeah," "Sure, Cody," "A cinch." Suddenly from distance a siren is heard. The light blinks off once. They all stiffen.

328.   CLOSE   VIC
his face impassive, but hopeful that this means help.

329.   INT. CAR   CLOSE ON BO CREEL   (PROCESS)   LATE AFTERNOON
His hand is close to the signal button as the siren comes closer. He glances into rearview mirror.

330.   INT. GAS TRUCK   MED. CLOSE   GROUP
Siren noise very close now. Cody has his gun out; other men are waiting, ready. They stare at light, waiting for signal. Suddenly it blinks once more. Slight pause. Then it blinks again, and a third time. They all relax. Vic frowns.

331.   EXT. HIGHWAY   FULL SHOT   LATE AFTERNOON
Bo slows truck, wheeling it over to side of highway as an ambulance reaches truck, speeds past. Bo presses down on accelerator. Truck gains momentum.

                                           DISSOLVE TO:

332.   INT. EVANS'S CAR   (CAR A)   LATE AFTERNOON
It is stationary. Evans sits beside driver, tensely watching operator in back seat. Suddenly operator hisses for quiet. Through headset comes faint rhythmic buzzing. As operator turns range finder, signal strength increases. When it is at its loudest:

CAR OPERATOR:
     Got 'em! (Into mike.) This is Car A at La Canada and
     Verdugo. Receiving signal. One zero five degrees.
     Will repeat . . .

                                           WIPE TO:

333.   INT. HEADQUARTERS   LATE AFTERNOON
Two agents stand before a large map of Los Angeles on

wall. They have plotting instruments and wait for the information being received by another agent who wears headphones and is receiving the messages as they come in.

AGENT WITH HEADPHONES (into mike):
Check. (Turns.) Car A at La Canada and Verdugo has a signal. One zero five degrees.

One of the standing agents draws a 105-degree bearing from intersection of La Canada and Verdugo.

FIRST AGENT:
Doesn't mean a thing till we get another bearing.

AGENT WITH HEADPHONES:
Ssh! (Into mike.) Come in, B.

334.   INT. CAR B
It is stationary. Here, too, a signal is being picked up. The operator in rear seat speaks rapidly into mike.

CAR B OPERATOR:
Car B at Valley and Garvey. Receiving signal. Three one six degrees.

335.   INT. HEADQUARTERS
as Car B's report comes through.

AGENT WITH HEADPHONES (into mike):
Check. (Turns.) Car B at Valley and Garvey. Bearing three one six degrees.

Second agent draws this bearing on map.

335A. INSERT   MAP
From the intersection of Valley and Garvey a line is drawn at 316 degrees. It intersects the first bearing on Colorado west of Allen in Pasadena.

335B.   BACK TO SCENE

SECOND AGENT:
Colorado west of Allen in Pasadena!

AGENT WITH HEADPHONES (into mike):
Source of signal—area of Colorado and Allen in
Pasadena! Will give general direction of route after
next bearings.

DISSOLVE TO:

336.   FLASH SHOTS   (IN MONTAGE EFFECT)   LATE AFTERNOON
1. The truck proceeding along a highway.
2. The occupants of the truck—CU's Vic and Cody.
3. The oscillator.
4. Direction finders turning.

DISSOLVE TO:

336A.   INT. EVANS'S CAR
in same location as before.

CAR A OPERATOR (into mike):
Car A. Bearing is now one three eight degrees.

336.B.   INT. HEADQUARTERS

AGENT WITH HEADPHONES:
Check. (Turns.) Car A bearing one three eight degrees. (Into mike, as this bearing is drawn on map.)
Come in, Car B. (Listens.) Check. (Turns.) Car B
bearing two eight four degrees.

Standing agents plot both these bearings from same car
positions as before. This time the lines intersect at Main
and Atlantic in Alhambra. The two points of location
are now joined with a thick line, showing direction.

SECOND AGENT (to agent with headphones):
Main and Atlantic in Alhambra! General direction
southwest.

336C.   INT. EVANS'S CAR
Evans has a map open on lap, pencil ready.

OPERATOR (listens; then into mike):
Check. (To Evans.) Source of signal Main and Atlantic in Alhambra. General direction southwest.

Evans draws line similar to one on big map.

EVANS (to driver):
Head southwest. (To operator.) Have Car B go southeast.

As car drives away at speed
DISSOLVE TO:

336D.   FLASH SHOTS   (IN MONTAGE EFFECT)
1. The truck.
2. The occupants.
3. The oscillator.
4. The FCC cars.

336E.   INT. EVANS'S CAR (A)

EVANS'S OPERATOR (into mike):
Car A at Western and Slauson. Bearing one five eight degrees.

336F.   INT. CAR B

CAR B OPERATOR (into mike):
Car B at Atlantic and Telegraph Road. Bearing two three five degrees.

336G.   INT. HEADQUARTERS
These bearings are drawn, intersection at Imperial and Figueroa.

SECOND AGENT:
Imperial and Figueroa.

AGENT WITH HEADPHONES (into mike):
  Source of signal Imperial and Figueroa.

DISSOLVE TO:

336H. FLASH SHOTS (IN MONTAGE EFFECT) LATE AFTERNOON
    1. The truck.
    2. Operators calling in new bearings (silent).

DISSOLVE TO:

336I. INT. HEADQUARTERS CLOSE
    The bearings being received and plotted on wall map and definite southerly direction down Figueroa now visible as a thick line continues to be drawn through all the points where bearings intersect (silent).
    DISSOLVE THROUGH TO:

337. INT. EVANS'S CAR CLOSE ON MAP IN EVANS'S HAND
    Pencil-marked similarly to larger map with route direction becoming more visible.

338. WIDER ANGLE IN CAR

    EVANS (looks up from map):
      Looks like the Long Beach area.

    CAR A OPERATOR (into mike):
      Car A at Rosencranz and Western. Bearing one five six degrees.

WIPE TO:

338A. INT. CAR B

    CAR B OPERATOR (into mike):
      Car B at Atlantic and Compton. Bearing two four four degrees.

WIPE TO:

338B. INT. HEADQUARTERS CLOSE ON MAP
    as the new bearings are drawn, intersecting at 198th and Figueroa.

183

FIRST AGENT:
> Source of signal One Hundred Ninety-eighth and Figueroa.

AGENT WITH HEADPHONES (into mike):
One Hundred Ninety-eighth and Figueroa.

WIPE TO:

339.　CLOSE ON SIGN　LOW ANGLE　　　　DUSK SEQUENCE
Shooting up at sign over enormous chemical plant which reads The Liberty Company, camera tilts down until it encounters forbidding wire fence, then dollies along this until it reaches a smaller sign: Warning! Keep Out! Pan around to street as the fourteen-wheeler makes a turn and approaches the guard's shack. Armed guard seen. A maintenance truck is seen disappearing into plant, gates closing after it. As the truck slows down guard steps out of the shack.

340.　EXT. AT TRUCK
as the guard comes in, Bo waves. Guard nods, pushes button; gates open. Bo drives into the plant. As gas truck disappears, pan around to show Verna's sedan parked in background across the street.

341.　EXT. CHEMICAL PLANT　ADMINISTRATION AREA
as gas truck stops near administration building. Bo alights, looks around quickly, sees that the area is deserted. He raps on the gasoline compartment. Out of the truck comes Cody, alone. He motions Bo to proceed ahead. Bo goes to door of administration building as others start to clamber out of truck.

WIPE TO:

342.　INT. EVANS'S CAR
which has moved to another location.

CAR A OPERATOR (into mike):
> Car A at One Hundred Sixty-sixth and Western.
> Bearing one three eight degrees.

WIPE TO:

342A. INT. CAR B

CAR B OPERATOR:
> Car B at Artesia and Alameda. Bearing two five six
> degrees.

WIPE TO:

342B. INT. HEADQUARTERS
The last two bearings when charted meet at the same
point of intersection as before.

FIRST AGENT (excitedly):
> Same as before—A Hundred Ninety-eighth and
> Figueroa!

AGENT WITH HEADPHONES (into mike; urgent):
> They must have stopped. A Hundred Ninety-eighth
> and Figueroa!

342C. INT. EVANS'S CAR

CAR A OPERATOR:
> Check. (To Evans.) A Hundred Ninety-eighth and
> Figueroa!

EVANS:
> That's it! (To operator as car whizzes sharp right.)
> Send out a call. All cars—proceed, a Hundred Ninety-
> eighth and Figueroa.[34]

WIPE TO:

343. EXT. ADMINISTRATION AREA
The last men are emerging from gas truck, carrying the
equipment. Cody leads them noiselessly up steps into
administration building, posting Cotton as lookout at
door.

344.   INT. OFFICE
Two desks, a few filing cabinets, and in background a large safe. A uniformed guard sits at desk playing solitaire, a tommy gun beside him. The upper half of the wall is glass, affording a complete view of corridor from inside office. Bo appears in corridor, comes to door, raps on glass. Guard looks up, frowning. Bo shows his pass, gestures his mission is urgent. Guard goes to door, peers through glass at Bo's identification card. Satisfied, he unlocks door. As he steps in, Bo raises a gun.

BO CREEL:
    Turn around.

As guard turns, Bo clips him viciously with butt of gun. Guard drops. Bo leans into hallway, beckons Cody and others in.

345.   ANOTHER ANGLE
as the men file in past Bo, going to their appointed positions (Het and Happy to safe with equipment). Vic is for a moment *face to face with Bo Creel*. Bo's jaw drops. Vic goes straight past him.[35]

346.   CLOSE   BO CREEL
Recognition snaps in his eyes. He moves swiftly to Cody's side, camera with him.

BO CREEL:
    Cody—that guy's a copper!

CODY (gasping):
    No . . . !

BO CREEL:
    I tell ya he's a copper! He's a T-man! His name's Fallon!

For a moment Cody stares uncomprehendingly at Bo. Then he whirls to face:

186

347.   VIC PARDO
He has taken advantage of the preceding moment to grab the guard's tommy gun, which he now levels at the men.

VIC:
Don't go for your guns.

348.   FULL SHOT
Cody merely stares, his mind momentarily refusing to assimilate the actuality of the betrayal. His eyes are glassy. The rest of the gang, gaping in consternation, look to Cody for orders. Then Cody starts to laugh, softly at first but becoming a hysterical outburst.

CODY (through laughter):
A T-man . . . How d'ya like that, boys? . . . A T-man . . . His name's Fallon . . . And we bought it . . . *I* bought it . . . Treated him like my kid brother . . . They must be waitin' to pin a medal on him . . . (Cannot stop laughing.)

VIC (hard):
Solid gold. Now if you're finished with your pretty speech, face the wall. All of you.

During this last, Cotton appears, seen through window in background as he comes swiftly toward office. He takes in the situation at once. Not by the flicker of an eye does Cody, or any of the others, give his presence away. Cody's continuing laughter drowns out any sound of footsteps.

CODY:
Yeah . . . A medal for the T-man . . . Only maybe he'll get it sooner than he thinks!

On cat's feet Cotton has edged up behind Vic, now slashes him across the temple with the butt of his gun. Vic drops. The laughter in Cody is gone. His gun comes down until it is pointing straight at the prostrate Vic's head.

COTTON (clutching him):
Cody, The joint's crawlin' with cops!

Slowly, Cody absorbs this, stares down at Vic; his gun hand drops to his side. Cody signals for Het to snap out the lights, moves swiftly to window, peers out through blinds.

349.   EXT. ADMINISTRATION AREA   (CODY'S ANGLE)
Deserted a few moments before, the area is now ringed with cars. Vague moving shadows can be seen as police and agents take up siege positions.

350.   CLOSE   CODY
A trap! But this isn't the end of Cody Jarrett. Not by a long shot. He signals for Tommy Ryley and Bo Creel to take vantage points on either side of the window. He moves stiffly to Vic, who stirs, groaning.

CODY:
Get up, copper.

BO CREEL:
Let him have it, Cody.

CODY:
And lose our ace in the hole? Uh-uh. The copper's gonna walk us outa here . . . ain't ya, copper? Get up. (He drags the groggy Vic to his feet.)

VIC:
It won't work, Cody. They'll shoot just the same.

CODY:
Coppers ain't gonna hurt one of their own.

VIC:
They won't make any deals.

CODY:
Ya better pray they do.

188

EVANS'S VOICE (through loudspeaker):
>   You're surrounded, Cody. You and your men might
>   as well give up.

Cody whirls, listening, eyes gleaming in the half-light.

351.   EXT. ADMINISTRATION AREA   BEHIND GOVERNMENT CAR
Evans holds a microphone to his lips. Behind cars nearby
crouch police and agents, ready to fire tear-gas guns.

EVANS (into microphone):
>   You haven't a chance. Come out with your hands
>   up.

352.   INT. OFFICE
Cody gestures for Cotton to stand guard over Vic. Then
he moves to window. With gun barrel he shatters a window.

CODY (calls out; harshly):
>   We got your boy Fallon in here! He'll be okay if ya
>   do what I tell ya!

353.   EXT. ADMINISTRATION AREA   FULL   FAVORING EVANS
His mouth tightens grimly. The other agents look at him.
A pause, as he debates with himself.

354.   PAN SHOT   VERNA AND T-MAN
Verna, held in a T-man's half–nelson, comes up to Evans, gasping, terrified.

T-MAN:
>   She says she can talk Jarrett out of it, Phil.

VERNA:
>   If I can, mister, will ya go easy on me?

EVANS:
>   Will you testify?

189

VERNA:
> I'll tell ya everything I know if ya go easy on me!

Evans hands her the portable mike.

VERNA (into mike):
> Cody—it's me—Verna—I fixed it up for ya, Cody. They don't want their guy hurt. Ya come out and they got a car for ya—they'll let ya get away—it's all set—

EVANS (angrily grabs mike; into it):
> She said that on her own! No deal! Now, either you come out or we come in after you. Talk, Jarrett. I'll wait ten seconds for your answer.[36]

He gestures for the men holding the tear gas to take aim at the window from which Cody has called out.

355.   INT. OFFICE   CLOSE ON CODY
Crouched at the side of the window, his answer to Evans's ultimatum is a demented cackle.

CODY:
> Come out with your hands up, the man says. How d'ya like that, Ma? Don't know who they're talkin' to, do they? (Shouting.) Here's my answer, ya dirty—

His words are cut off by shots from his gun.

356.   EXT. ADMINISTRATION AREA
as the shots tear into the steel of the ringed cars. The besiegers crouch behind them out of harm's way, but Verna, late in ducking, is hit. One glance tells Evans she is dead. Grimly, he gestures to the men with tear-gas guns. They raise their heads above the hoods of the cars behind which they are crouched, take aim.

357.   INT. OFFICE   CODY
His mind has snapped almost at the moment that he squeezed the trigger. He yells exultantly.

CODY:
   That was Cody Jarrett talkin'!

The window shatters as three tear-gas bombs explode in the office. Mushrooms of blinding smoke envelop the men. Coughing, choking sounds are heard. Cody, in his unreason, momentarily unaffected even by the gas, whirls toward where Vic was lying on floor. His view is obscured by the smoke.

CODY:
   Now it's your turn, pal.

He fires into smoke. A man's mortal scream is heard. Now the fumes get to Cody and tears stream from his eyes; he chokes, his breath rattling as he gulps for air.[37]

358.   CLOSE   LOW ANGLE   VIC AND COTTON
   barely discernible in the swirling, blinding smoke. It is Cotton, standing guard over Vic, who has been fatally hit by the burst from Cody's gun. He falls across Vic, who grabs his gun and crawls into a corner, pulling a handkerchief from his pocket and holding it over his mouth. The remainder of the men, blinded, tears coursing down their faces, coughing, stumble out past him into the corridor.

359.   INT. CORRIDOR   GANG
   as they stumble out. Tendrils of tear gas drift out into corridor. Cody exits last, tears streaming down his cheeks. He stands as if dazed.

BO CREEL (grasping Cody by arm):
   The side door, Cody. We can make a break for it.

Cody allows himself to be led by Bo down corridor toward side door. They are followed by Happy, Het, and Ryley. Pan to office door as Vic, choking, picks himself up and drags himself to door. He stands there, breathing in deep draughts of clean air.

359A.   SIDE DOOR   ADMINISTRATION AREA
Cody motions to Het and Happy to go out first, as though
they were a reconnaissance team. Pan with them as they
stealthily walk out. As Bo, Cody, Ryley, and the Reader
start to follow, several yards behind, Happy and Het are
mowed down by machine-gun fire. Cody, Bo, Ryley, and
the Reader duck back through the door into the corridor.

359B.   INT. CORRIDOR   THE GANG
Bo, followed by Cody, Ryley, and the Reader, runs down
the corridor toward rear door. Bo starts to open door.

360.   EXT. ADMINISTRATION BLDG. AREA   LATE EVENING
Police and T-men converging area from right and left.
They stand ready with guns. (They do not cover rear
door.)

   EVANS:
      Fan out!

360A.   EXT. REAR DOOR   LATE EVENING
It bursts open and the gang breaks out.

360B.   POLICE AND T-MEN   LATE EVENING
They are attracted to the rear door and start firing.

361.   REAR DOOR EXT.   LATE EVENING
Gang returns fire as they start running. An answering
burst of fire from off-screen drops Bo Creel. The remaining members of the gang, seeing their escape cut off,
veer around the corner of the building into the protective labyrinth of the plant itself.

362.   EXT. AT GOVERNMENT CARS   LATE EVENING
Evans races in.

   EVANS:
      Don't fire unless you've got a clear target. This place

is a stack of dynamite. (To an agent.) Get the fire department.

The men move cautiously toward rear of plant. Pan to rear door as Vic comes out, waving handkerchief. Evans recognizes Hank and hurries to him. (NOTE: Vic will henceforth be known as Hank Fallon again.)

EVANS:
Are you all right, Hank?

HANK (nodding):
Get a car out to Charlie's Roadhouse—Highway Sixty, near Colton. Pick up Daniel Winston. He's the man we're looking for—the fence.

EVANS (calling off):
Frank!

An agent comes up.

363.   EXT. POLY AREA   MOVING SHOT   LATE EVENING
Cody, followed by Ryley and the Reader, staggers into the welter of pipes, tubes, and motors. They pause. Cody leans against a generator, looks back.

364.   WHAT HE SEES
Vague shadows closing in on the poly area. The Reader hides behind a large piece of tubing, preparing to make a break.

365.   EXT. MOVING SHOT   CODY   LATE EVENING
followed by Ryley. The knowledge that the law is closing in gives Cody new strength. He exchanges fire, turns, staggers through a further labyrinth of turbines, generators, and pipes. He and Ryley climb up a short metal ladder across a catwalk and then down again.

366.   EXT. FULL SHOT   GOVERNMENT MEN   LATE EVENING
They are closing in. By now they are beginning to look like shadows.

367.   MED. SHOT EXT.   CODY AND RYLEY   LATE EVENING
They break out of poly area again. Cody stares around
wildly like a hunted animal. He sees superfraction area
with its protective superstructure. He motions to Ryley
and they both head for it. The shadows are now deep-
ening. Night is rapidly approaching.

368.   EXT. BOILER AREA   READER   ALMOST DARK
runs into poly area, is spotted by an agent off-screen,
who fires at him. Reader returns the fire.

369.   GOVERNMENT AGENT   EXT. BEHIND TANK   ALMOST DARK
He takes aim, fires at the Reader off-screen.

370.   EXT. CLOSE   THE READER
He is hit and falls.

371.   EXT. FOLLOW SHOT   CODY AND RYLEY NEAR SUPERFRACTION
AREA   ALMOST DARK
They take refuge for a moment behind a door. Cody leans
against it, exhausted. He looks off-screen.

372.   OMITTED

373.   EXT. GROUP OF CARS   EVANS, FALLON, AND OTHERS
Police and agents pour out of cars. Pan quickly to another group of cars from which more agents and police
run out.[38] We see equipment and searchlights being set
up and tested, ready for use.

374.   OMITTED

375–76. EXT. CODY AND RYLEY AT SUPERFRACTION AREA
                                              ALMOST NIGHT
They move slowly with the desperation of men on whom
the net is closing. Searchlights begin playing in the opposite direction.

CODY:
> It's getting dark. We'll make our break now.

He nudges Ryley to follow him, pointing toward Hortonsphere area. Camera follows them as they arrive at base of Hortonsphere. Cody starts up the steps as Ryley lags behind, hides by a large pipe. As Cody continues up the steps he hears:

RYLEY'S VOICE (off-screen):
> Don't shoot! Don't shoot! (Cody wheels around, stares down, his eyes searching.)

377. **WHAT HE SEES RYLEY IN BEAM OF SEARCHLIGHT NIGHT**
his hands upraised, coming slowly forward toward light.

RYLEY (mumbling in terror):
> Don't shoot! I'm coming out.

378. **CLOSE ON CODY** **NIGHT**
He raises his gun.

379. **FULL SHOT** **NIGHT**
Ryley, still in searchlight beam, coming toward T-men, his hands upraised. A shot is heard. Ryley is hit, sinks to the ground. The agents wheel toward source of shot.[39]

380. **CODY** **NIGHT**
He runs down the ladder of the Hortonsphere and starts running up ladder of another one. It is only the strength of madness that keeps him going. In running from one Hortonsphere to another he exchanges a few shots.

381–83. **SIDE OF HORTONSPHERE CLOSE ON CODY NIGHT**
He scrambles up the ladder which is seen to wind around the steel bulbous sides. He stumbles up—up—up—as the rays of searchlight hit him. He empties his gun right into the rays of searchlight. The light goes out. He continues to climb to the top of the Hortonsphere.

384.   TOP OF HORTONSPHERE   NIGHT
As Cody reaches it he realizes, dimly at first, that he has
reached a dead end. There is no way down but the ladder he climbed. Voices off-screen, drawing closer. Weaving slightly, aware now he has chosen his own death-
trap, he stands astride top of Hortonsphere, which is
like the globe itself. He stands there alone, naked and
unprotected, challenging the world in his madness.

385.   ON GROUND NEAR HORTONSPHERE   NIGHT
Evans and Fallon stand beside two cars, stare up. They
know where Cody is. Evans hands Fallon the gun with
a snooperscope.

       HORTONSPHERE   FROM THEIR ANGLE   NIGHT
Now it is even more like a globe—the earth itself—with
a lone, tragic figure standing atop it, claiming it, refusing to admit defeat.

       EVANS'S VOICE:
            You might as well come down, Jarrett. There's no
            one left but you.

386.   TOP OF HORTONSPHERE   CODY   NIGHT

       CODY (glares down; still cocky, still top man):
            Come and get me!

387.   EVANS AND FALLON   ON GROUND   NEAR HORTONSPHERE
       (SHOOTING OVER FALLON'S SHOULDER)   NIGHT
Fallon brings up snooperscope, sighting Cody. Camera
dollies through up to sight, and from this point on to
end of scene we see the action in the sight of snooperscope by infrared. We hear a shot fired. Cody is hit.

388.   OMITTED

389.   CLOSE SHOT   FALLON AND EVANS   NIGHT
Fallon still looking through sight and firing. He hits Cody
again.

FALLON (to Evans):
> What's holding him up?

390. TOP OF HORTONSPHERE   CODY   NIGHT
Another bullet tears into his chest. He staggers, bites his lips against the surging pain. He realizes he's through.

CODY (hoarsely):
> Anyway, Ma, I made it . . . Top of the world!

He is now out of his mind. He staggers against the rail, trying to shoot back at what hit him. Instead his bullets hit the pipe valve which holds the gas in the tank under pressure.

391. HORTONSPHERE   MED. CLOSE   CODY   NIGHT
He is pumping slugs into the pipe. We hear sound of escaping gas. Suddenly the gas is ignited from the blast of Cody's gun and Cody is completely enveloped in flames.[40]

391A. ON GROUND   FALLON, EVANS, AND OTHERS   NIGHT
camera pans with them as they start running away from the flaming area. Off-screen sound of terrific explosion. The area is all lit up as they continue to run for cover.

391B. FULL SHOT   EXPLOSION   (STOCK)   NIGHT

391C. HORTONSPHERE AREA   (STOCK)   NIGHT
Flames consuming what was once a cluster of Horton-spheres. Fire hoses playing on the fire, etc.
> DISSOLVE TO:

392. CLOSE-UP   EVANS AND FALLON   (FIRE IN BACKGROUND—PROCESS)   NIGHT
They look at fire, say nothing. Then:

EVANS:
> One man against the world.

FALLON (shakes head):
    Why do they try? . . . Why do they try?[41]

392A.   FULL SHOT   FIRE (STOCK)   NIGHT
                                            FADE OUT

THE END[42]

Notes to the Screenplay

1 The fireman's pleading line is not in the film.
2 Cody's line in the film: "Maybe tomorrow or maybe in the spring. I'll give it a lot o' thought. All right? Mmm. Smells good, Ma."
3 Director Raoul Walsh shot scene 36 differently by beginning with a tight close-up of Verna still asleep (see figure 3).
4 Verna's line in the film: "What else does a girl do around this bear trap?"
5 Dialogue in scene 44, it is interesting to note, is practically verbatim in the film, with only minor variations.
6 Scenes 52–53 were set in a snow-covered landscape in the Temporary version of the script. When Zuckie stumbled and fell, unconscious, he was buried by a gathering snowfall. According to screenwriter Ivan Goff, Warner Brothers objected to the production costs of a wintry scene, so the cabin-hideout scenes were altered to suggest bitter cold but not snow. The revised scenes 52–53 may or may not have been filmed, but they do not appear in the final version of *White Heat*.
7 The wall photograph of the President—perhaps because the President was now Harry Truman, who was less popular at Warner Brothers than FDR—does not appear in the film.
8 Scenes 65–69 are dated as being completed by May 17, 1949.
9 In the Final version of the script the movie playing at the drive-in is a Warner Brothers musical, identified as *Silver Lining*. (Scenes 103–113 are dated May 17, 1949.)
10 The Temporary version of the script contained a maudlin exchange at this point:
  MA JARRETT: What'll ya do without me, son? What'll happen to ya without your old Ma?
  CODY (gruffly): Don't worry, Ma. Maybe it won't be as long as you think. I'll be on my good behavior. That's the one place it pays off . . . in prison.
  MA JARRETT (brokenly): Cody . . . Cody! With you gone it'll be like night all the time . . .
11 Scene 115 to this point is dated May 17, 1949. Revisions for the rest of 115 and scenes 116–21 are dated June 10, 1949. Scene 120 is labeled "Already Shot."

12 Dialogue for scenes 115B–117B was substantially altered in the film. The actual dialogue introducing scene 115B:

FALLON: Hello, Phil. How's the arm?

EVANS: I'll live. Ah, you're lookin' good.

FALLON: Yeah. (Laughing.) It's that prison diet. Great chef in San Quentin. I hated to leave.

EVANS: You did a whale of a job.

FALLON: Aw, most talkative little con I ever shared a cell with.

EVANS: That whole syndicate comes up for trial in a few weeks.

FALLON: Yeah?

EVANS: Oh, what's that?

FALLON: You put it on a pole, wind a spool of silk thread around it, and you hold the pole over the water. Then you sit under a nice shady tree and relax. After a while a hungry fish comes along, takes a nip at your hook, and you've got dinner. For the next two weeks I'm not gonna think about anything except the eternal struggle between man and the fish. I've been promised a vacation, you remember?

EVANS: Sorry, Hank. That's out.

13 In the Temporary version of the script, this Fallon-Evans exchange forms a subtext:

FALLON: How about that coffee?

EVANS: Sure. (Quietly, as he pours coffee.) I should've got him, Hank.

FALLON: Don't worry. We'll get him.

EVANS: *You'll* get him.

FALLON (looking at him): What difference does it make?

14 In the Final version of the script, Cody does reply: "Tough enough."

15 At this point in the Temporary version of the script there is an interior scene in Evans's office with Evans, Margaret Baxter, and a photo-technician. Evans is giving Baxter, an actress, final coaching before she visits Fallon in prison, posing as his wife. The technician takes her photograph to set up scene 141, which survives in the film.

16 The first portion of scene 157 may or may not have been filmed by director Walsh, but in the film the scene begins with Ma Jarrett's final speech to the assembled Jarrett gang.

17 The film adds an exquisite character detail here, probably suggested by Walsh. Just before kissing Verna, Big Ed spits out his chewing gum, a bit of business later repeated by Verna, with some irony, when she kisses Cody just before they embark on the oil refinery heist. An interviewer once asked Walsh about this detail:

Q. Did you strive for realism in your films? In *White Heat*, for instance, before Mayo and Cochran kiss, they spit out their gum. Did you introduce a touch like that?

A. Sometimes you had time—the clouds would come up or something would have to be changed on the set—and you'd start thinking about little pieces of business for the actors. But otherwise you had to go so damn fast you didn't stop for a gum-chewing scene. ("Can You Ride the Horse?" An interview with Raoul Walsh by James Childs, *Sight and Sound* [Winter 1972–1973], p. 9.)

18 Walsh shot scenes 204–206 in a single take. Likely as a consequence, there are numerous permutations in the film dialogue.

19 Scenes 206–10 are dated June 7, 1949.

20 Margaret's actual reply: "Perfectly clear. You won't be sorry, Vic. When you get out, we'll be happy. I'll see to that." This parting line of dialogue is all that remains of the sexual possibilities between the characters of Fallon and Margaret Baxter, as per early drafts of the script. Even at that, as filmed by Walsh and as acted by Edmond O'Brien, the remark passes in the film without any intimation of its original design.

21 At this point, the Temporary version of the script contains a scene between Evans and his wife, Mary. Mary is worried about the risks and demands of Evans's job and complains that being married to him is "like being married to a test pilot." This anxiety between husband and wife was one of the subplots eliminated as the script developed.

22 Significantly, the "trembling, abject" Cody Jarrett of the Revised Final is not the one acted by Cagney in the film. That Cody is struggling and screaming and has to be physically subdued before being led away by the guards as the scene ends. Evidently, this is one of the nuances Cagney contributed during the filming.

Walsh filmed scene 229 more effectively, closing with a long, master shot of the prison mess hall. The convicts, after being shocked into silence, are slowly resuming activity as Cody Jarrett, in his garbled fury, is dragged from the site.

23 At this point, the Temporary contains an additional prison visit between Fallon and his "wife" with Fallon relating the news of Cody Jarrett's breakdown. It concludes with Fallon's sexual come-on, "When I get out, I was wondering if—tell me, do you have any prejudices against ex-convicts?"

24 Scene 238 is dated May 17, 1949.

25 Scenes 258–60 are dated May 17, 1949.

26 In its earliest manifestation (from the Temporary) this memorable

line was, "Stuffy, huh?" followed by the shooting of Parker in the car trunk. During filming Cagney gave it one final twist: "Oh, stuffy, huh? I'll give yuh a little air."

27 In the Final version of the script, there is additional dialogue at this point before Big Ed is gunned down:
BIG ED: You sure wanted to live, didn't you, sugar?
CODY: What's that mean?
Verna quakes.
BIG ED (a grim smile): Nothin'. (Over his shoulder.) What are you waiting for?

28 Walsh shot this slightly differently than indicated. The door is not so much half-opened as it is slipped ajar by Cody, whose half-lit visage is revealed by the camera.

29 Big Ed is actually *buried* by Cody and the Jarrett gang in the Temporary version of the script. While the dirt is being piled on the grave, Cody is heard to murmur, "It's okay now, Ma . . . "

30 Scenes 296–300 are dated May 17, 1949.

31 The dialogue in the film:
VIC: Well, anyway, she quit runnin', Cody.
CODY: Yeah, quit runnin'. That was a . . . it was a good feelin' out there, talkin' to 'er. Just me and Ma. Good feelin'. I liked it. Maybe I am nuts. Let's go in and have a drink.

32 Scene 303 to this point is dated May 20, 1949. In earlier drafts of the script, Verna is not present in this scene between Cody and Vic.

33 In the film Cody's tag line, probably improvised on the set, is an improvement: "Grab the brass ring . . . " It is spoken as Verna is riding monkey-style on Cody's back, giggling drunkenly, and reaching for a bottle of champagne on a table.

34 Scenes 328–342C, including some marked as already shot, are dated June 13, 1949.

35 Walsh shot this differently than indicated in the script, with Bo Creel (Ian MacDonald) not recognizing Fallon until both are in the room and at opposite ends of the office, keeping watch. The change is a subtle improvement and heightens the suspense.

36 The exchange in the film:
POLICEMAN: She says she can get Jarrett to come out.
VERNA: If I can, mister, will you go easy on me? I'll tell 'im you'll let him get away because you don't want your guy hurt. He'll believe me. And when he comes out you can do what you want with 'im.
EVANS: No deal.

ASSISTANT: Lock her up.

VERNA: You cheap copper.

Also, Verna is *not* killed by a stray bullet in the first exchange of gunfire, but is led away safely—presumably to prison.

37 Pages from this point to the end of the screenplay are dated June 3, 1949 (in the last week of filming).

38 In the film, Evans has a line of dialogue here, transposed from scene 362, that foreshadows the ending: "All right. Pass the word along. Don't fire unless you've got a perfect target. That place is a stack of dynamite. Have that area surrounded. Get some searchlights." This is followed by Cody's rambling, berserk utterances: "They think they got Cody Jarrett! They haven't got Cody Jarrett! (Etc.)"

39 In earlier versions of the script, Ryley (Robert Osterloh) is the sole surviving gang member, the only one to surrender without being killed.

40 The screenwriters tinkered with various endings during the development of the script, including one in the Revised Temporary version of the script in which "Cody's body falls against the railing, tumbles over. It glides heavily down the side of the Hortonsphere, almost like a figure on a slide in a fun house, then suddenly it is unsupported, plunging lifelessly through the air, hitting the ground with a sickening crash. Cody Jarrett is dead."

41 The last lines in the film are:

CODY: Made it, Ma! Top of the world.

EVANS: Cody Jarrett!

FALLON: He finally got to the top of the world and it blew right up in his face!

42 Scenes 31, 54, 55, 71, 76, 87, 93, 235 and 323A, are dated June 18, 1949—after principal shooting. They are pick-up shots done largely by an auxiliary crew.

31. AT TUNNEL JARRETT GANG covering Zuckie lying on tracks.

WILD LINES:
"What happened?"
"Zuckie got scalded."

CODY:
"Let's get out of here."

54 INSERT INDICATING "TAHOE COUNTY MORGUE"

55.   PAN SHOT   LOS ANGELES   FINISHING ON SHOT OF FEDERAL BUILDING reading:

> ## LOS ANGELES FEDERAL DISTRICT

DISSOLVING TO:

a door marked:

> ## U.S. TREASURY DEPARTMENT
> ## LOS ANGELES DIVISION
> ## PHIL EVANS

71.   REAR END OF MA'S CAR WITH MARKER ON BUMPER CAMERA PULLS BACK
as Evans's car drives up to curb behind Ma's car.

76.   SHOT FOR MA'S CHASE   SHOT OF CAR C (Ford) MAKING FIRST RIGHT-HAND TURN TO PICK UP MA'S CAR.

87.   SHOT OF MA'S CAR FOLLOWED BY CAR C (Ford).

93.   PAN SHOT   ANOTHER SECTION OF LOS ANGELES WINDING UP ON INSERT OF MILLBANK MOTEL
getting over point that this is San Fernando Valley.

235   DOCTOR (into phone):
Dr. Simpson speaking . . . Yes, Warden. I just finished my report on Jarrett. Violent. Homicidal. He'll probably have recurrent periods of normal behavior but . . . Yes, sir—the psychiatrists are coming tonight. They'll commit him to the Institution . . . Yes, Warden . . . I suggest you prepare the release for him . . . Thank you, Warden.

323A.   SHOT OF POLICE LIEUTENANT PHONING EVANS.

POLICE LIEUTENANT. (holding sheet of paper in his hand): Radio signal—Fallon. Do you know what that means, sir?

(This after man tells gas station attendant that mirror in washroom is dirty.)

Production Credits

Produced by	Louis F. Edelman
Directed by	Raoul Walsh
Screenplay by	Ivan Goff and
	Ben Roberts
Suggested by a story by	Virginia Kellogg
Director of Photography	Sid Hickox, A.S.C.
Art Director	Edward Carrere
Film Editor	Owen Marks
Sound by	Leslie G. Hewitt
Set Decorator	Fred M. MacLean
Wardrobe by	Leah Rhodes
Special Effects by	Roy Davidson, Director
	H. F. Koenekamp, A.S.C.
Orchestrations by	Murray Cutter
Makeup Artist	Perc Westmore
Music by	Max Steiner
Assistant Director	Russell Saunders

Running time: 114 minutes
Released: September 1949

Cast

Cody Jarrett	James Cagney
Verna Jarrett	Virginia Mayo
Hank Fallon (Vic Pardo)	Edmond O'Brien
Ma Jarrett	Margaret Wycherly
"Big Ed" Somers	Steve Cochran
Philip Evans	John Archer
Cotton Valetti	Wally Cassell
Het Kohler	Mickey Knox
Bo Creel	Ian MacDonald
The Trader	Fred Clark
The Reader	G. Pat Collins
Roy Parker	Paul Guilfoyle
Happy Taylor	Fred Coby
Zuckie Hommell	Ford Rainey
Tommy Ryley	Robert Osterloh
Chief of Police	Marshall Bradford
Ernie Trent	Ray Montgomery
Police Surgeon	George Taylor
Willie Rolf	Milton Parsons
Cashier	Claudia Barrett
Popcorn Vendor	Buddy Gorman
Jim Donovan	DeForrest Lawrence
Ted Clark	Garrett Craig
Judge	George Spaulding
Clerk	Sherry Hall
Guards	Harry Strang, Jack North
Russell Hughes	Sid Melton
Margaret Baxter	Fern Eggen
Nat Lefeld	Eddie Foster
Tower Guard	Lee Phelps

This comprehensive cast list is from Homer Dickens, *The Films of James Cagney* (Secaucus, N.J.: Citadel Press, 1972), p. 188.

Inventory

The following materials from the Warner library of the Wisconsin Center for Film and Theater Research were used by McGilligan in preparing *White Heat* for the Wisconsin/Warner Bros. Screenplay Series:

Treatment, by Virginia Kellogg, no date, 34 pages.
Treatment, by Kellogg, October 16, 1948, 31 pages. Research material, July 2, 1948, 4 pages.
Treatment, by Ivan Goff and Ben Roberts, November 9, 1948, 20 pages.
Temporary, by Goff and Roberts, March 10 to March 12, 1949, incomplete, 130 pages.
Revised Temporary, by Goff and Roberts, April 8, 1949, 136 pages.
Final, by Goff and Roberts, April 20 to April 23, 1949, incomplete, 94 pages.
Revised Final, by Goff and Roberts, May 4 with revisions to June 18, 1949, 130 pages.

WW

The Wisconsin/Warner Bros. Screenplay Series, a product of the Warner Brothers Film Library, will enable film scholars, students, researchers, and aficionados to gain insights into individual American films in ways never before possible.

The Warner library was acquired in 1957 by the United Artists Corporation, which in turn donated it to the Wisconsin Center for Film and Theater Research in 1969. The massive library, housed in the State Historical Society of Wisconsin, contains eight hundred sound feature films, fifteen hundred short subjects, and nineteen thousand still negatives, as well as the legal files, press books, and screenplays of virtually every Warner film produced from 1930 until 1950. This rich treasure trove has made the University of Wisconsin one of the major centers for film research, attracting scholars from around the world. This series of published screenplays represents a creative use of the Warner library, both a boon to scholars and a tribute to United Artists.

Most published film scripts are literal transcriptions of finished films. The Wisconsin/Warner screenplays are primary source documents—the final shooting versions including revisions made during production. As such, they will explicate the art of screenwriting as film transcriptions cannot. They will help the user to understand the arts of directing and acting, as well as the other arts involved in the film-making process, in comparing these screenplays with the final films. (Films of the Warner library are available at modest rates from the United Artists nontheatrical rental library, United Artists/16 mm.)

From the eight hundred feature films in the library, the general editor and the editorial committee of the series have chosen those that have received critical recognition for their excellence of directing, screenwriting, and acting, films that are distinctive examples of their genre, those that have particular historical relevance, and some that are adaptations of well-known novels and plays. The researcher, instructor, or student can, in the judicious selection of individual volumes for close examination, gain a heightened appreciation and broad understanding of the American film and its historical role during this critical period.